# STUDENT'S BIBLE ATLAS

*Edited by*

## H. H. ROWLEY

*Cartography by John Callow, B.A., F.R.G.S. a.. Cedric E. Bush*

# Contents

## LUTTERWORTH PRESS
### CAMBRIDGE

First published 1965
Fifteenth impression 1996


The Lutterworth Press
P.O. Box 60
Cambridge
CB1 2NT

## ACKNOWLEDGEMENTS

Lutterworth Press wish to acknowledge the valuable assistance given by
the following:
Rt Revd Mgr John M T Barton, Rev E F F Bishop, Rev H Wakelin Coxhill,
Miss Frieda M Dearing, Professor John Foster, Dr Stewart W Herman, Mr
Benson Y Landis, Dr H C Lefever, Rev Basil Minchin, Dr Cecil Northcott,
Rev James Sutton, Dr Henry P Van Dusen and Dr Marcus Ward.

In addition reference was made to *Karte der Religionen der Erde*
published by Evangelisher Missionsverlag of Stuttgart and
Geographisher Verlag Kümmerly & Frey of Berne.

British Library Cataloguing in Publication Data:
A catalogue record is available from the British Library.

ISBN 0 7188 0896 7

Printed by Midas Printing (UK) Ltd.

# INTRODUCTION

*(*indicates that a name will be found in the Index of Place names)*

## 1

## GEOGRAPHY OF PALESTINE

THE PURPOSE of a Bible Atlas is to enable the user to understand the Bible better. For geography exercises a powerful influence on history, and much in the Bible, and especially in the Old Testament, cannot be understood fully, save in its geographical setting.

Palestine is a remarkable country. Its length " from Dan to Beersheba " (Jg. 20: 1) is only about 150 miles, and its greatest width not more than about half as much. Yet it has exercised an influence on mankind out of all proportion to its size. It lay at the western extremity of the " Fertile Crescent " (which is the cultivated area at the northern end of the Arabian peninsula and included the valleys of the *Tigris and *Euphrates and Syria and Palestine to the border of Egypt); and it formed a bridge between the ancient empires of Mesopotamia and Asia Minor and that other cradle of Near Eastern civilization, Egypt. Its political power was never very great, though its people often dreamed of political greatness; but the great empires with which it was surrounded recognized the political importance of the control of this bridge. The Israelites long felt the cultural and religious pressures of the subdued Canaanite population, as the Old Testament makes plain. They also felt the influence of their neighbours and conquerors, including the Persians, the Greeks, and the Romans (see Maps 7–12), throughout their history.

Despite this, Palestine has had a greater and more enduring influence on the world than any other comparable area. Its material culture was not notable. Its surviving literature in the Bible has been translated into innumerable languages and is widely treasured. Yet it is not treasured for its literary merit, great though that is, but for its religious quality and message. This is not derived from Israel's environment, but from her own experience of God and His power. Her religious leaders were men who brought no message of their own devising, but who spoke what they profoundly believed to be God's word and not their own. Yet that message cannot be understood without reference to the geography and history of the land. The geography influenced the history, and the message of God's spokesman was often addressed to the concrete situation of the moment. For Biblical religion is always related to life, both individual and national. It was never simply a matter of worship at a shrine. It called men to worship God and also to hear His voice, directing them in all their ways, and bringing them the assurance that in obedience to Him lay their true well-being.

### Natural Divisions

Geographically, Palestine is a most varied land. Moving from west to east it is divided into four regions:

(1) First, there is the coastal plain, which includes the Plain of *Philistia and the Plain of *Sharon to the point where Mt. *Carmel juts out into the sea, and then the Plain of *Acco and *Phoenicia to the north. At the southern end the plain rises in the *Shephelah towards the hill country of Judah.

(2) Running from north to south through the land is a highland ridge, broken in places by belts of lower country. In the south is the hill country of Judah, rising to over 3,000 feet. Separated from it by a belt of lower hill country is the central highland, or hill country of Ephraim, with Mt. *Ebal and Mt. *Gerizim standing on either side of *Shechem. Separating this area from the hills of *Galilee is a break in the hills, running from south of Mt. *Carmel to the River *Jordan, known at its western end as the Plain of Esdraelon and at its eastern as the Valley of *Jezreel. South of the Valley of Jezreel stands Mt. *Gilboa. The hills of Lower Galilee, which include Mt. *Tabor, not far from *Nazareth, are not so high as those of Upper Galilee, which lead on to the *Lebanon. Here the coastal plain is very narrow, and this explains why the Phoenicians always looked to the sea and became a great seafaring nation. South of the hill country of Judah is the Negeb, which lay between *Beersheba and *Kadesh-barnea, though not very closely defined. Its poor rainfall made it unsuitable for cultivation, but it provided grazing land.

(3) The third division of the land is the *Jordan Valley, which lies in a deep cleft that divides Eastern from Western Palestine and continues down to the *Red Sea. The sources of the Jordan lie in the *Lebanon and *Anti-Lebanon mountains, and it flows through the *Sea of Galilee to the *Dead Sea. The former is nearly 700 feet below sea level and the latter some 1,300 feet below. Between the Sea of Galilee and the Dead Sea the river follows a very winding course and in parts its banks are well wooded. As it nears the Dead Sea the valley of the Jordan widens out. Here stands *Jericho in an area where the heat becomes very great, and where the vegetation is almost tropical. The Dead Sea has no outlet and its water is very salty, so that it can support no life. On its south-eastern side is a peninsula, known as The Tongue, and south of this the sea is much shallower. On the west of the Dead Sea lies the *Wilderness of Judah, where David sought refuge from Saul at *Engedi, and where the Dead Sea Scrolls have been found at *Qumran and *Murabba'at. The rapid fall from the hills of Judah to the Dead Sea may be seen from the fact that from the old city of *Jerusalem to *Jericho the road descends more than 3,000 feet in a distance of 14 miles in a direct line. South of the Dead Sea lies the *Arabah (Dt. 2: 8), which rises above sea level and then falls again to the Gulf of *Aqaba.

(4) The fourth division is on the east of the Jordan. This is a high plateau, divided by four rivers, the *Yarmuk, the *Jabbok, the *Arnon, and the *Zered. The Arnon and the Zered flow through deep gorges, which greatly accentuate the divisions of the land. North of the Yarmuk lay *Bashan, and beyond this the Anti-Lebanon, with Mt. *Hermon, whose snows can be seen from the *Sea of Galilee. Between the Yarmuk and the Jabbok lay the country of Gilead, and between the Jabbok and the Arnon the country of Gad and Reuben, though this was often overrun by the Ammonites from the east. Here stood Mt. *Nebo, from which Moses viewed the Promised Land (Dt. 34: 1ff.). Between the Arnon and the Zered lay Moabite territory, and south of the Zered lived the Edomites.

## Influence of Geography on History

From this brief glance at the outline of the country light is shed on its history. So many natural barriers are found that communications were very difficult, and it was hard to maintain political unity throughout the area. One main road ran through the land, and this was used by the warring armies of Israel's neighbours in times of conflict and by trading caravans in times of peace. It ran from *Damascus through *Galilee, then across the plain and out to the coast south of *Carmel and down through the coastal plain to the borders of *Egypt. *Judah lies off this road, and so Judah was less influenced by the international stream of people who passed through the land. The Jordan had few good fords, and so the country east of the river was much isolated, while its own natural obstacles made political union difficult even in this area.

The coast of Palestine has no good natural harbours. For long periods the Philistines controlled the southern part of it, and sometimes extended their sway into the Plain of *Sharon. So it is not surprising that the Hebrews never became a seafaring people. Apart from the Jordan and its tributaries, there are few rivers in the land. Many of the river beds became dry except after the rains, when they were rapidly swollen, as happened to the *Kishon (Jg. 5: 21). The chief rains fell in the autumn and the spring, but the amount of rain decreased from north to south. Hence water was very precious, and in *Jerusalem and elsewhere it was preserved in cisterns (Jer. 2: 13) beneath the houses. Outside Jerusalem there was a spring, and before David captured the city (2 Sam. 5: 6ff.) water was brought by a tunnel from this spring to a point from which people in the city could draw it up through a rough shaft cut in the rock. But there was danger of the water being diverted by an enemy in war, and therefore Hezekiah brought it by a tunnel into the lower part of the city (2 Kgs. 20: 20) to the pool of *Siloam.

2

# THE STORY OF THE BIBLE

HAVING LOOKED at the land, we must look at the Bible and the way it has come to us, before we discuss the history which it records. To describe in a few paragraphs how we got the Bible is no easy task. Three processes have to be remembered: the composition of the individual books; the gathering of the books to form the Bible, or the formation of the Canon; and the transmission of the text through the centuries.

## The Composition of the Books of the Bible

It is plain that the authors of many of the books used older sources. Some are quoted in the Pentateuch (Num. 21: 14), Joshua (Josh. 10: 12f.), Samuel (2 Sam. 1: 18ff.), Kings (1 Kgs. 14: 19, 29), and Chronicles (2 Chr. 24: 27). The authors of some of the books used ancient traditions which had been faithfully handed down. These sources and traditions carry us far behind our present books. The prophetic books were not compiled by the prophets whose names they bear. They undoubtedly contain genuine oracles from these prophets and reliable fragments of their biography, but for their present form we are indebted to the disciples of the prophets or later compilers. In the New Testament we have four Gospels, of which the first three are clearly related to each other. We know that other Gospels were written (Lk. 1: 1ff.). We have the book of Acts, which is a continuation of the Gospel of Luke, and which preserves for us part of the story of the Early Church. There is much more which we should have liked to know. Most of the twelve disciples are unmentioned in it, and of the story of Peter we know little after the conversion of Cornelius (Acts 10). We have a number of Letters, in which we can trace the setting out of Christian teaching and see something of the life of the churches, and have glimpses of some of the individual Christians of the apostolic age.

But the human processes by which these various books came into being are not the whole story. Just as God was active in the history which will be outlined below and revealed Himself in the texture of the story, so He was active in the writing of these books. They came into being over a very long period, and there are great diversities in them. Yet there is also a very remarkable unity. It is the same God who is active in the story of both Testaments; it is the same God who reveals Himself and His will in both. His signature is seen everywhere, and the great purpose of the study of the Bible is not to learn the history, but to see and hear the God who speaks in the Bible, and to bring to Him the response of obedience.

## The Formation of the Canon

The hand of God is to be found not only in the writing of the individual books, but in their collection to form the Bible. The earliest collection in the Old Testament to be accepted as sacred was the Pentateuch. Precisely when it reached its present form is not known, and different scholars have different ideas. It must have been before the Samaritan breach with the Jews (4th cent. B.C.), for the Samaritans have the same Pentateuch and hold it sacred. Since they do not have the other books of the Old Testament, with the exception of a variant form of the book of Joshua, it is probable that the same sacredness did not attach to them at the time of the breach. This does not mean, of course, that they had not been written. When the second division of the Jewish Canon, the books from Joshua to Kings and the prophetic books, with the exception of Daniel, became so sacred that no other books could be added, we do not know. But it is certain that they were accepted as sacred by the beginning of the second century B.C. because of the use that was made of them in the Hymn in praise of the Fathers in Ecclesiasticus 44ff. By that time other books were already being treasured, though it was still possible for more to be added, and ultimately these became the third division of the Jewish Canon. By New Testament times it is probable that the collection, substantially as we have it in Hebrew now, had been gathered together and was accepted as sacred. For in Lk. 11: 51 Jesus refers to the blood that was shed from the blood of Abel to the blood of Zechariah. The reference here appears to be to 2 Chr. 24: 20ff. 2 Chronicles is the last book in the Hebrew Bible, so the meaning seems to be " from the beginning of the Old Testament to the end," and the end was what it is now.

At the end of the first century A.D. the Rabbis gathered together at Jamnia and there they discussed what books should be reckoned as Scripture. They discussed whether Ezekiel and the Song of Songs should be so regarded. Clearly they did not regard the limits of the Canon as fixed. But it is significant that they did not consider whether any new book should be brought in, but whether any book should be rejected, despite the wide acceptance it had had. Ezekiel had already been accepted in Ecclesiasticus 49: 8. The fixing of a Canon is the end of a process, and not its beginning. It is when books have been treasured for so long that they cannot be surrendered, and when there have been no additions for so long that it seems impossible to add others, that the Canon becomes fixed by tacit consent so that it can then become fixed by a decision. It is clear that the Old Testament had been so fixed by tacit consent before the Rabbis met at Jamnia, since the books of the Hebrew Canon of the Old Testament have always been in the Bible of the Church.

In the oldest Christian manuscripts of the Old Testament, which are written in Greek, some additional books, not found in the Hebrew Old Testament, are found. Some were certainly Jewish books, written originally in Hebrew, and the Christians must have received them from Jews who regarded them as sacred. Yet that recognition never became established, and we have no evidence that any of these books were accepted as canonical by the Rabbis at Jamnia or so much as discussed by them. Some of these books are to be found in the Apocrypha, and with them is 2 Esdras, which is not in any of these Greek manuscripts and which has not come down to us in Greek. Among the oldest manuscripts no two agree in the list of additional books included. It is, therefore, improper to speak of them as belonging to a Canon at this stage. In the manuscripts they are not put together, but scattered among the other books, which are not in the same order here as in the Hebrew.

Gradually additional books, not in the Hebrew Canon, came to be widely accepted as belonging to the Bible. Not all the early Church Fathers accepted them, and there have always been voices raised against them. In the sixteenth century, at the Council of Trent, the Roman Catholic Church declared these additional books to be canonical, and in Catholic Bibles they are found scattered as in the early manuscripts. Some of the Reformers accepted them as profitable for reading, but not as canonical, while others rejected them altogether. When they are found in Protestant Bibles, they stand together between the Old Testament and the New under the title of Apocrypha. But the books of the Old Testament are not restored to the order of the Hebrew Bible, and hence 2 Chronicles is not the final book of the Old Testament.

The process of canonizing the New Testament was similar to that of the Old. Books were treasured because they were valued by individuals and churches, until gradually the same collection was widely treasured before there was any specific decision. The lists of books given by early Church Fathers are not all the same, and some include books not now in the New Testament, such as Hermas and the Didache. Some reject Hebrews, and Revelation was challenged until a late date in the East, though it was early accepted by the Western Church. But by the end of the second century the list of New Testament books given by Irenaeus is substantially the same as we now have. He does not include 2 Peter, 3 John, James, Jude, or Hebrews, but he does include Hermas.

Human processes, therefore, went into the forming of the New Testament Canon. But again there is a unity running through the books, binding them together despite their diversity. They present the same Christ, who lived and taught and died and rose again in Palestine, and whose death and resurrection were interpreted as the means of salvation wherever the Gospel was taken. The New Testament is not a casual or haphazard collection of books, but a collection of books that truly belong together.

Moreover, the Old Testament and the New Testament belong together. The New Testament could not be understood without the Old; and the Old Testament without the New is broken off, looking to something beyond itself, without which it is incomplete. The New Testament takes much in the Old Testament for granted and not needing to be repeated. The Old Testament formed the Bible of the Church before there was a New Testament, and the New Testament responds in remarkable ways to the hope and promise of the Old. Above all, the two Testaments contain the record of the revelation of the same God to His chosen people, Israel. Not all Israel received the second part. But the Old Testament had itself spoken of the Remnant that should respond in faith and obedience and should inherit the promises, and the Church began as a Remnant of Israel which received the new revelation of God, given with the same manifest marks of His hand as the old. The Old Testament had a place for those not of Israel according to the flesh who became members of the true Israel by faith and obedience, and Judaism had accepted proselytes and recognized them as heirs of the promises. The Church with eagerness sought to win both Jews and Gentiles who should enter into the New Israel and share its faith and blessing.

## The Transmission and Recovery of the Text

The text of the Bible has been transmitted to us by the pious labours of Jews and Christians. For centuries both Testaments were copied by hand, and every copyist is liable to make mistakes. It is not surprising, therefore, that there are innumerable differences in the manuscripts. Yet the number of important differences is remarkably small. The problems created by the text of the two Testaments are very different. For the Hebrew of the Old Testament we are dependent on Jewish manuscripts. Until recently the oldest major manuscripts of the Old Testament were of the tenth century A.D. or later. At some time prior to that the text had been fixed, and the words and even the letters in each book counted to provide tests of the accuracy of the copying. While there are many small variations in the manuscripts, they are for the most part in agreement. But many centuries of copying had gone on before the text was fixed. We now have from the *Qumran caves some major manuscripts of books of the Old Testament not later than the first century A.D., and fragments of every book of the Old Testament with the exception of Esther, while from *Murabba'at, a few miles south of Qumran, we have fragments of other manuscripts, dating from not later than the second century A.D. These latter manuscripts agree almost entirely with the later manuscripts which give the fixed text. Some of the Qumran manuscripts agree closely with this, but others include a number of readings which were known to us previously in the Septuagint (see below), and yet others which differ from both of these forms of the text. It would, therefore, seem as if the text was fixed around A.D. 100, and that before this manuscripts were liable to vary more one from the other. But between the composition of the books of the Old Testament and the fixing of the text there was a long period, during which errors could come in.

The earliest Christian Old Testament was the Greek version, known as the Septuagint. Some of the New Testament writers must have used the Hebrew Old Testament, but the Gentile Church needed a Bible in Greek. Where the New Testament quotes the Old, it sometimes agrees with the Hebrew, sometimes with the Septuagint, and sometimes not quite with either. The Septuagint version was made by Jews, and its earliest parts were translated in the third century B.C. It was made from Hebrew manuscripts, but since it differs widely from the Hebrew fixed text it bears witness to a variant form older than the fixed text. From the Septuagint the Old Latin version was made. Other Greek versions were made from the Hebrew by Theodotion, Aquila, and Symmachus, and in the fourth century A.D. Jerome made a new Latin version, known as the Vulgate, from the Hebrew. Translations from the Hebrew into Aramaic (Targums) and Syriac (Peshitta) were also made. To use these various versions to get behind the Hebrew fixed text to the original text is far from easy. Sometimes the translations were free, sometimes they seem to have misunderstood the text they were translating. And we have to remember that they were subject to errors as they were copied and recopied.

In the case of the New Testament our earliest Greek manuscripts come from a date much nearer the date of composition than in the case of the Old. A fragment of John's Gospel comes from not later than the first half of the second century A.D., and a number of other early fragments are known. Major manuscripts still exist in the great Uncial texts of the fourth and fifth centuries, and vast numbers of later manuscripts are known. Versions in Latin, Syriac and other languages have also to be considered here, and the problems of the New Testament textual scholar, while different from those of the Old, are intricate and complex.

Many of the translations of the Bible into modern languages were made before some of our present materials were known, and before scholars had begun the scientific study of the materials even then available. This will explain why so many new translations are being made in our day. They are made because Christians believe it is important to get as near as we can to the original form of the books that comprise the precious collection of the Bible. Often we must remain in uncertainty, and scholars disagree on this reading or that. Yet rarely does anything vital for our faith rest on the uncertain texts. Here, once more, therefore, while we must recognize human factors in the transmission of the text, as in the composition of the books and the gathering together of the Canon, we may find the hand of God guiding the pious hands of the copyists, and preserving for us and for the generations that shall follow the record of His wonderful gifts in grace.

# 3

# THE BIBLE AS HISTORY

THE BIBLE contains much history; yet it is not a book of history, but of religion. It was not compiled to record the history of Israel, but to set forth the acts of God which took place in and through Israel's history. The Egyptian historian would take little account of the release of some slaves under Moses, but to the Biblical writers this was of supreme importance because in this deliverance from bondage God had claimed Israel for Himself in a unique way. He had revealed His own character as a compassionate and a saving God, who rightly claimed Israel's worship and obedience because of what He had done for her. Similarly, Herod's recorders would not notice the massacre of a few children or the escape of one to Egypt, and no historian of that time would record the crucifixion of a Galilean carpenter. These events are important to the writers of the New Testament because they belong to the history of salvation. The child who escaped was God's supreme revelation of Himself, and His death and resurrection were the divine means of a wider salvation, effective for all men, and making its claim on men everywhere for a response in worship and obedience.

## The Importance of Bible History

It is sometimes thought that since the history is recorded for its message it is immaterial whether it is actual history. A parable does not have to be history to be spiritually profitable. Nevertheless, it is of the highest importance that the great events through which God is said to have revealed Himself should be true. The faith of the Bible is not something that men thought up, and not something for which we have merely to take their word that it came from God. Moses came to Israel promising them deliverance in the name of God, and then deliverance was wrought by powers that Moses could not control and did not profess to control. Moses claimed nothing for himself, but interpreted the deliverance to the people and led them to commit themselves to the God who had delivered them. Here it is of the greatest importance whether this deliverance is historical or not. Though it is not recorded in any ancient source outside the Bible, there is ample reason from the account itself to believe it. No people would invent the story that they had been slaves if they had not. And no people would suppress the story of their own might or cleverness if they had fought their way to freedom or by cunning brought it about. Similarly, it is a matter of great importance whether Jesus actually lived, or whether He was crucified and rose again. In both Testaments these are the actual events within which revelation and redemption are to be found.

## Archaeology and Bible History

It is often claimed that archaeology has proved the historical accuracy of the Bible. This is rarely true. Few items of Biblical history are recorded also in secular history. But, what is more important, archaeology (see Map 6) has in many ways increased our confidence in the Biblical record. It has brought new information which perfectly fits in with the Biblical account, while it has immensely enriched our knowledge of the background of Israel's history and illustrated what is recorded there. Sometimes, and particularly in relation to the Exodus, it has made the task of the Biblical student more difficult. It is impossible here to write in detail of the history of Israel, but a rapid survey may make some things clear. Before the time of Abraham *Egypt and *Babylonia were highly civilized, and archaeology has brought to light abundant remains of their civilization in the form of material objects and historical and other records. Abraham once lived in *Ur, in Babylonia, and then in *Haran, in northern Mesopotamia, before he moved to *Canaan. Israelite law has behind it a background of ancient Near Eastern law, represented in various Sumerian and Babylonian law codes now known to us. Many customs which are reflected in the patriarchal stories are true to Mesopotamian life about 1,500 B.C., as we find it represented especially in the finds at *Nuzu, though these customs do not appear in later Israelite practice. We therefore know that the patriarchal stories are true to the way of life of the ages in which the patriarchs lived. If tradition has correctly preserved the customs of a past age, it is probable that it preserved also the substance of the story. With all this we have to remember that the spiritual quality of the story of Abraham is not copied from Babylonia, and if our respect for the historical value of the stories is increased, we may have confidence, too, in their spiritual truth.

## The Exodus from Egypt

Of Israel's stay in Egypt or of the Exodus we have no account from Egyptian sources. But there is a great deal of information from Egyptian and other sources which fits in well with the Biblical story (see Map 3). The Egyptian empire was sometimes extended through Palestine to the *Euphrates, and the *Amarna letters were written by Palestinian princes to their Egyptian overlord before the Settlement of the Israelites. From these and from other Egyptian sources there is much that is relevant to the question of the Exodus. The name of the Pharaoh of the Oppression is not preserved for us in the Bible, but we are told that the Israelites were set to taskwork at *Pithom and *Raamses (Ex. 1: 11), while elsewhere in the Bible the deliverance from Egypt is connected with *Zoan (Ps. 78: 12, 43). Zoan is the Hebrew form of the name Tanis, the later name of the ancient city of Avaris. This was rebuilt by Rameses II and for a short period bore the name of Pi-Ramesse, which is preserved in the name Raamses. Here we have some pointer to the date of the Oppression, and so of the Exodus, and another example of the tenacity of Hebrew tradition.

There is no reason to doubt the fact of the Exodus, or the subsequent commitment of Israel to the God who had delivered her. Attention has been drawn to the fact that in the form of the covenant of Israel with God there is much similarity to Hittite treaties, which gave control over other states, from about 1500 B.C. Both here and in the similarity of Hebrew legal codes to other ancient codes, we should not overlook the unique elements which are found in Israel. The Hebrews may have built on older foundations, as every generation must, but the building was a new one. Living where she did in the age in which she did, it was inevitable that much in the civilization in which she was set should appear.

## The Period of the Judges

When the Israelite tribes entered Palestine, they were surrounded by Canaanites, who were not all destroyed (Jg. 1: 21, 28, 30, 32; 2: 23), and who continued to control many of the more important cities. Only gradually did the Israelites gain the upper hand (see Map 4). Meanwhile they lived side by side with the Canaanites, and the Bible makes it clear that often they copied the customs and the worship of their neighbours. Of the culture and religion of the Canaanites we have much fuller knowledge since the discovery of the Ras Shamra tablets on the site of the ancient city of *Ugarit. Although this lay in the far north of Syria, it almost certainly represented a local variety of the general situation of Syria and Palestine, and we see with greater clearness why the higher elements in Israel fought against the Baal cult, which was corrupting the religion they had brought with them from *Sinai. The battle was a long one, and it is surprising that it was not lost altogether in the period that followed the Settlement. The Israelites had no continuous leadership in the tradition of Moses through all that period. There were attacks of Midianites or Ammonites, or conflicts with the Canaanites or the Philistines, and often the tribes were in conflict with one another. Their leaders were successful warriors who in the name of the national God led them against their foes. The powerful neighbour states of Egypt and Mesopotamia were not active in Palestine in this age, and the field was left to the local conflicts among the little states that made up Palestine with the region east of the Jordan.

## The Early Monarchy

It was under the pressure of the Philistines that the Israelite monarchy came into being. These non-Semitic invaders gradually pushed their way up the coastal plain. They drove the Amorites before them so that they in turn pressed the Danites (Jg. 1: 34), until they were forced to seek another home in the north (Jg. 18). Then the Philistines pressed on inland, until they were in dominant positions in the very heart of Israel at *Geba (1 Sam. 13: 3) and controlled all the working of iron in the land (1 Sam. 13: 19ff.). This oppression must have been felt and resented as much by the Canaanites as by the Israelites. But it was Israelite prophets who fired the hearts of the people with patriotic zeal, and when the prophet Samuel urged Saul to take the lead against the enemy (1 Sam. 9: 16; 10: 7) he was assured of support. Ammonite pressure on *Jabesh-gilead (1 Sam. 11) gave Saul the opportunity to gather his forces for a venture which the Philistines would not oppose, since it was not directed against them. Its success gave Saul an opportunity to turn on the Philistines and drive them from the heart of the country. The victory at Michmash (1 Sam. 14) was won through Jonathan's intimate knowledge of that area, near which he had lived all his life. It enabled him to scale the face of the rock and to throw the Philistine outpost into panic, which soon spread through the army.

The Philistines tried to press up the narrow valleys into Judah but were checked (1 Sam. 17), and were unable to restore their position until the end of Saul's reign. By then they had established their power in the whole of the coastal plain and across the lower country north of the central highlands as far as *Beth-shan. Then they attacked Saul from the north, and at *Gilboa the Israelites were defeated and Saul and Jonathan were slain (1 Sam. 31). Saul's son, Ishbosheth, retired across the Jordan to *Mahanaim, while in the south David became king at *Hebron (2 Sam. 2: 1ff.). Again the Philistines did not interfere, since David was a dependant of the king of *Gath (1 Sam. 28: 1ff.), and he did not seem to menace them. But when Ishbosheth was killed (2 Sam. 4: 5ff) and David was accepted as king over all Israel, the position was changed. It was too late now, however, and David soon established his rule over the Philistines (2 Sam. 5: 17ff.). Prior to this he had captured the stronghold of *Jerusalem (2 Sam. 5: 6ff.), which had remained in Jebusite hands so far. It is possible that David had been hampered in his conflict with Ishbosheth by the Jebusites. For while Canaanites and Jebusites would not hamper the Israelites in the conflict with the Philistines, they would hardly be well disposed to David while he was a dependant of the king of Gath.

The power of David was now great enough to reduce his neighbours on other sides, and when he died he left Solomon ruler of the greatest empire Israel ever had, though it was small compared with the other empires of the ancient Near East (see Maps 7–12). The internal difficulties of the surrounding countries provided the opportunity which was now seized. None of the greater neighbours was able to interfere in Palestine in the time of David. But his empire soon crumbled. Solomon did not have to fight for his kingdom, and was able to organize it for the support of a considerable court, but lost the hearts of his people in the process. He taxed the trade that flowed through the peaceful roads of his country and developed with Tyrian aid sea trade from the Gulf of *Aqaba, since he controlled the country between Palestine and *Ezion-geber.

## The Divided Kingdom

Before Solomon's reign ended, his weaker hand had let most of David's empire slip away from him (see Map 5). The Philistine menace no longer welded the people together, and after the death of Solomon the Disruption of the kingdom took place (1 Kgs. 12). The small states which David had conquered were now independent, and for a long period there were conflicts, either between the two Israelite kingdoms or between one or other of these and their non-Israelite neighbours. These continued until Assyria began to press toward the west, and Egypt, aware of the menace to her borders, intrigued with the Palestinian and Syrian states to check Assyria. For a short time Egypt had been allied with Solomon (1 Kgs. 9: 16), but a change of dynasty in Egypt made that country the refuge of Solomon's enemies (1 Kgs. 11: 17, 40), and after the Disruption Shishak had led a raiding expedition into Palestine. The Bible tells us only of his treatment of Jerusalem (1 Kgs. 14: 25ff.), but his own inscription makes it plain that he harried the northern kingdom also. But after that Egypt took little part in Palestinian affairs for a long time.

In the ninth century, however, Assyria was extending her power in the west. At that time northern Israel and *Damascus were engaged in frequent conflicts, and in one of them Ahab won a victory which placed Benhadad, the king of Damascus, in his power (1 Kgs. 20: 33). He angered the prophets by making a treaty with Benhadad, for which the Bible does not tell us the reason. From an inscription of Shalmaneser III we learn that shortly after this the Assyrian army met a coalition of Syrian and Palestinian states, in which the armies of Benhadad and Ahab fought side by side, at *Qarqar. Here the Assyrian advance met a check.

Soon after this there was revolution in Israel. Omri, a strong ruler who seized power in Israel and who founded the dynasty which continued through four reigns, had formed an alliance with Tyre. His son Ahab had married Jezebel, a Tyrian princess (1 Kgs. 16: 31), who actively promoted the worship of the Tyrian god in Israel. This roused the prophets, and brought about Elijah's conflict with the prophets of Baal on Mt. *Carmel (1 Kgs. 18), and led to the downfall of the dynasty. The prophets fomented revolution and brought the house of Jehu to the throne (2 Kgs. 9: 1ff.). From Assyrian sources we learn that Jehu speedily gave tribute to Assyria, doubtless to strengthen his position, since he had lost the Tyrian alliance.

There followed a period of Assyrian inactivity in the west, which was marked by local strife among the small states there, until the end of the century, when Assyria subdued the Damascus state. This opened the way to the prosperity of northern Israel in the reign of Jeroboam II. For Assyria was again not active in the west and Damascus had not recovered its former strength, and Israel attained a prosperity it had not known since the Disruption. In Judah, too, under Azariah, or Uzziah, there was a similar growth in strength. But prosperity brought new evils, and the prophets Hosea and Amos condemned all the evils that were rampant in the northern state. Its end, indeed, was not far off. After the death of Jeroboam there was no settled monarchy, but frequent revolutions. Assyria was now pressing towards the west once more, with a new ruthlessness when Tiglath-pileser came to the throne. Egypt was also fomenting trouble, so that there was a pro-Egyptian party and a pro-Assyrian party in the country (Hos. 7: 11). Damascus fell to Assyria in 732 B.C., Samaria fell in 721 B.C., and the northern kingdom was at an end (2 Kgs. 17: 1–8).

Judah survived this crisis. Before the fall of Damascus Israel and *Aram had tried to force Judah into the alliance against Assyria (Isa. 7), but Ahaz had appealed to Assyria for help. Judah now stood in a greater peril, with Assyria on her doorstep; and Egypt, conscious of the menace to her own borders, redoubled her efforts to hold Assyria back. To judge from the prophecies of Isaiah and Micah, social and religious conditions in the south were no better than in Israel. By the end of the century Hezekiah had been drawn into an alliance against Assyria, and had brought down upon himself and his country the might of Sennacherib's armies. We learn from Sennacherib's inscriptions that Hezekiah had forced *Ekron into the alliance and had imprisoned Padi, its king, in Jerusalem. Sennacherib ravaged the country and shut Hezekiah up in Jerusalem. But the city was delivered. Sennacherib was forced to withdraw by plague in his army, described in the Bible as the angel of the Lord (2 Kgs. 19: 35f.; cf. 2 Sam. 24: 15).

There followed the long reign of Manasseh, in which Judah remained subject to Assyria. Assyrian arms were carried into Egypt, which was for a time subdued. But by the end of the reign of Manasseh the days of Assyria's greatness were over. Attacks from over the Caucasus had weakened her, and at the end of the reign of Ashurbanipal in 626 B.C. *Babylon rebelled. During the remaining years until the fall of *Nineveh to the combined forces of the Babylonians and the Medes in 612 B.C. there were frequent changes of kings, and Assyria was in no position to interfere in the west.

This gave the opportunity to Josiah to assume independence and to spread his power into Israel. His reform of religion (2 Kgs. 22f.) was the religious side of his bid for independence. It was checked not by Assyria, but by Egypt. In Assyria's hour of danger, as we learn from the Babylonian Chronicle, Egypt became her supporter and sent troops to help her. After the fall of Nineveh the Assyrian capital was transferred to *Haran, which fell two years later. Now Egypt sought to claim for herself all the Assyrian empire west of the *Euphrates. When Josiah opposed her at *Megiddo, it cost him his life (2 Kgs. 23: 29), and Egypt controlled the succession to the throne. In 605 B.C. the Egyptian armies were routed at *Carchemish, and Judah came under Babylonian power. But Egypt continued to scheme, and it was the conflict between Egypt and Babylon which supplies the key to the political history of Judah until the fall of Jerusalem.

## From the Exile to the Advent

In 597 B.C. Jerusalem fell to Nebuchadnezzar, when Jehoiachin surrendered and was taken captive to Babylon (2 Kgs. 24: 10ff.). Tablets stating the rations which were allowed to him and his five sons still survive. In 586 B.C., following a new revolt, Jerusalem was taken and destroyed after a long siege, and the *Temple was laid in ruins, while large numbers of the people were taken into exile (2 Kgs. 25: 1ff.). That exile lasted until the end of the Babylonian empire, when Cyrus seized that empire and in 537 B.C. gave permission to the Jews to return (Ezr. 1: 1ff.). Many did not return, but those who did found great discouragement as they sought to renew their life in Palestine. There was tension between those who had remained in the land and those who returned, and though the Temple was rebuilt (Ezr. 5f.), the period immediately after the exile was not notable for its civil or religious history.

In the fifth century the walls of Jerusalem were rebuilt under Nehemiah (Neh. 6: 15) and the religious life of the Jews was reorganized under Ezra (Ezr. 7: 1ff.). This century was marked also by growing tension between Jerusalem and Samaria. The breach was not yet absolute, for at the end of the century the Jewish community at *Elephantine, in Egypt, appealed to both Jerusalem and Samaria for help to secure permission to rebuild the temple of Yahu, i.e. Yahweh.

Little is known of the history of the Jews in the fourth century B.C. During this century the Persian empire fell and Alexander rose to power (see Map 11). We have considerable knowledge of these events from non-Biblical sources but little from Biblical. Alexander passed through the land to Egypt, where he founded *Alexandria, a city in which there were many Jews from the start. After the death of Alexander in 323 B.C. his empire was divided among his generals, who soon established their independence of one another and fell to fighting among themselves. In time there emerged three main divisions of his empire, of which two concerned the Jews. The Ptolemies ruled Egypt, while the Seleucids ruled *Syria, Asia Minor and Babylon, and claimed control over the regions farther east which they were not able to enforce. Before the battle of *Ipsus, it was agreed between Ptolemy and Seleucus that Palestine should belong to Egypt, but Ptolemy's forces did not arrive until after Antigonus had been defeated, and Seleucus claimed that the agreement was void. Meanwhile, however, Ptolemy had occupied Palestine, and for a century it remained in Egyptian hands, though it was frequently claimed by the

Seleucids. In 198 B.C. Antiochus III defeated Egypt at the battle of Panion (near *Caesarea Philippi), and thereafter Palestine was transferred to the Seleucids. A few years later Antiochus lost Asia Minor to *Rome, and was forced to pay a large sum of money.

Soon, internal disagreements among the Jews, and especially on their attitude to Greek culture and influence, and the strong hellenizing policy of Antiochus IV, led to dire troubles for the Jews. These were aggravated by various causes. Seleucid taxation was heavy, and Seleucus IV, the brother and predecessor of Antiochus IV, had attempted to rob the Temple. Antiochus IV was not the rightful heir, and there were some who disputed his title. Soon he began to appoint his own nominees to the office of high priest. In addition, Antiochus was deeply humiliated by the Roman envoy in Egypt, and ready to vent his anger on someone. He therefore launched an attack on the Jewish religion, knowing that if he could destroy the religious root of opposition, the political root could not survive. This attack led to the revolt of the Maccabees, which in the end led to Jewish independence under the Hasmonaean dynasty, and this lasted to the time of Herod the Great. By that time Rome had appeared on the eastern Palestinian scene, and the Seleucid kingdom had fallen. Pompey marched through Palestine and soon Egypt was added to the Roman empire (see Map 12).

With great skill Herod, whose father, Antipater, had secured considerable influence in Judea under the later Hasmonaeans, steered his way through all the difficulties of the Roman Civil War, and maintained his influence with whoever was in the ascendant, until Rome gave him the title of king over a country he had to win. Within a short time he had established himself as the king of Palestine, owing allegiance to Rome. His immense building enterprises, including the complete rebuilding of the Temple, and his ruthlessness are well known. At his death his kingdom was divided by the emperor, and the title of king was given to none of his family. Judea and Samaria were given to Archelaus, but ten years later he was removed by the Romans and his territory put under a procurator, responsible to the governor of Syria. Throughout our Lord's ministry Pilate was the procurator, and it was he who ordered the Crucifixion.

During the period from the Maccabean rising, the Jewish religious leaders had formed into two parties. The Pharisees were the heirs of the stricter Jews of Maccabean days, but they were themselves divided into the more liberal wing of Hillel and the more conservative wing of Shammai. The Sadducees were led by the powerful priests, wealthy and worldly. Most of the common people belonged to no party. There were other special groups and of one we have knowledge from the Dead Sea Scrolls, which were found in the neighbourhood of *Qumran and which came from a very pious and exclusive sect. This sect appears not to have shared in the Temple worship because the high priestly line of Zadok (1 Kgs. 1: 45) no longer continued. The members cherished messianic hopes, and among their special writings they treasured one which looked forward to a triumphant war against all the kingdoms of the world. It seems likely that they are to be identified with the Essenes, of whom Josephus and other first-century writers tell us, though in their own writings we see them at an earlier date.

## From the Advent to the Fall of Jerusalem

Herod Antipas, the tetrarch of Galilee (Lk. 3: 1), who imprisoned John the Baptist and had him beheaded at *Machaerus (Mk. 6: 17ff.), was banished by the emperor to Gaul in A.D. 39, when he sought the title of king. This title had already been given to Herod Agrippa I, who had succeeded Philip and Lysanias (Lk. 3: 1). Later, the Roman procuratorship of Judea was ended and this area was added to the kingdom of Agrippa. But when he died, his son, Herod Agrippa II, was given the rule over a small area in the north, and procurators were again given the authority. But Agrippa II had a residence in Jerusalem and was given authority over the Temple. It was before him that Paul made his defence (Acts 26). Felix and Festus, before whom Paul appeared (Acts 24f.), were successive procurators of Judea. From the beginning of the first century A.D. there had been a growing hostility towards the Romans among many Jews, and an eager expectation of the coming of the Messiah, who, it was hoped, would destroy the Roman power and begin the age of Jewish dominion. A party known as the Zealots had been formed, pledged to throw off the Roman yoke. Extremists among them, known as *sicarii*, employed the weapon of murder. In the year A.D. 66, when Florus was the procurator, the seething unrest burst into revolt against Rome, and the Jewish War, which ended in A.D. 70, began. It seems likely that the Qumran sect was allied with the Zealots in this conflict; for the Romans destroyed their headquarters at Qumran. Some of the Zealots withdrew to *Masada, and maintained a stubborn resistance there until A.D. 73.

## The Meaning of the History

Looking back over this history it would seem that Israel was always a pawn—sometimes a pawn among pawns and sometimes a pawn among kings, but always a pawn. Her land was the meeting place of empires, and it was impossible not to be involved in their affairs. Yet, speaking of such situations as we have outlined, the prophets were sure that if Israel were obedient to God, she might walk fearless through all the perils. God could bring her out of Egypt by His might alone. He could send the storm to turn the plain into a sea of mud and halt the chariots of Sisera. He could send plague into the armies of Sennacherib. In any situation He could preserve Israel's well-being. This does not mean that the response of the prophets to every situation was the same. Deborah could summon the people to battle (Jg. 4: 4ff.); Isaiah could counsel quiet confidence in the face of Sennacherib's insolent threat (Isa. 30: 15); Jeremiah could counsel submission to Nebuchadnezzar (Jer. 38: 17ff.).

The prophets believed that if the nation walked with God His wisdom would direct their way. But they were sure that when men did not walk with God they could not have His wisdom. All the social ills that they denounced were the proof that men were not walking with

God. For walking with Him meant reflecting His character. He was compassionate, righteous, and full of grace, and therefore those who stood in covenant with Him must show the same compassion, righteousness, and grace towards all who stood in the same covenant with them, if they were to walk with Him. Israel's well-being was not the reward she would earn by her conduct. It was the free gift of His grace, and her conduct was but her response to that grace. When she withheld her response she broke the covenant and withdrew herself from God. Yet it is not to be supposed that by well-being material prosperity is always meant. Prosperity could be corrupting, as it was in the days of Solomon and of Jeroboam II. When men obeyed the will of God then He was with them to preserve all their truest interests, and it was His presence which constituted their ultimate well-being. He was with Joseph in the prison (Gen. 39: 21) as truly as when he was exalted.

### The Early Spread of the Church

So far our thought has been limited to Palestine. But New Testament history carries us beyond its borders. For the Early Church soon spread from Jerusalem to *Samaria, *Caesarea, *Damascus and *Antioch, and from there Paul set out on his missionary journeys. He owed much to the history briefly outlined above. Wherever he went, he was within the Roman empire (see Map 12), using the roads that Rome had built, and, despite his many sufferings, owing not a little to the peace and order which Rome maintained. From the establishment of Alexander's empire (see Map 11) the Greek language had been widely understood, and Rome had not replaced its use by Latin. Indeed, Greek was much used in Rome itself. Hence, wherever Paul went, he was able to make himself understood in the Gentile world by using Greek. Wherever he went, too, he found Jewish synagogues and places of prayer. For in the post-exilic period Jews were found not only in Alexandria, but in little communities scattered through the Mediterranean world. Associated with them were proselytes from the heathen, who had committed themselves completely to the faith of Israel, and many others who were more loosely attached. For despite the exclusiveness of Judaism, large numbers of converts had been made. Wherever Paul went, he found his first opportunity to preach the Gospel in these Jewish places of worship, and though he was often cast out and persecuted, he often took with him a group out of which a Church was formed (see Maps 15-17).

Of the light shed by archaeology on the life of Paul, a single instance may be noted. At *Corinth Paul was brought before the proconsul Gallio (Acts 18: 12ff.). An inscription found in Delphi enables us to date his proconsulship in the year A.D. 51-52 or A.D. 52-53, and most probably the former. This helps us to fix the dates of the events of Paul's ministry. It also sharply reminds us how rapid was the early spread of Christianity. Within about twenty years from the Crucifixion the Church had spread through Syria, Asia Minor, and Greece. When we remember how few the disciples were at the time of the Crucifixion, and that they included no powerful or wealthy men, we are astonished at the speed of the Church's spread, despite strong opposition and persecution (see Map 18). If every small group of Christians today had the same strong missionary purpose, we should see great things.

Our story began with the call of Abraham and God's deliverance of Israel and revelation of His character and will. It has carried us through the changing course of Israel's history, set between empires and subject constantly to alien influence, but addressed by men of God. These constantly recalled her to the great principles of her faith, and interpreted the will of God in terms of the social and political conditions of their day, teaching her that the greatest deliverance is the deliverance from evil and that God's law is to be written on men's hearts (Jer. 31: 31ff.). It has brought us to the time when the supreme revelation of God was given and when the divine power for the deliverance of all men was released in the death and resurrection of Christ, and to the time when that message was carried forth from Jerusalem to Rome. It has reminded us of the varied preparation for this final act in the story of salvation, and of the part that geography and world history played in the story. It has also reminded us that history and geography alone do not explain the story. The hand and the voice of God belong to it. We have been carried to the time when the Temple was destroyed and Jewish sacrifices came to an end. But before that day God had provided a better sacrifice, and already before the destruction of the Temple the Church had recognized that no other sacrifice was necessary for salvation.

## 4

## THE WORLDWIDE EXPANSION OF THE CHURCH

THE STORY of the Church from New Testament times to today cannot be compressed within a brief section (see Maps 19-24 and Time Charts 1 and 2). Yet, since this Atlas is intended for use in Churches which have come into being as the result of the modern expansion of the Church, something should be said.

### The Church Persecuted

The book of Acts carries us to *Rome and leaves Paul in prison. Whether he was released or what he did afterwards, if he was, we cannot know with any assurance. That he was martyred in Rome during the reign of Nero is almost certain. But the expansion of the Church did not end there. Christians continued to make Christians wherever they went, and in the second century there was a Church in France and in Egypt and North Africa, as well as throughout the area visited by Paul. Quite early there was a Church in *Edessa, and tradition says that Thomas carried the Gospel to India and China. In India there is still a Church which claims to have been founded by him. The missionary expansion of the Early Church was quite incredible, and it was largely achieved by the spreading of the flame of faith from individual to individual. As Augustine put it: " One loving soul sets another on fire."

This is the more surprising when we remember the persecutions that the Early Church had to face. From the time of the Neronic persecution in A.D. 64, following the Great Fire of Rome for which the Christians were made to take the blame, to the time of Constantine's Edict of Milan in A.D. 313, the Christians were liable to face persecution and a cruel death in some part of the Roman empire. The two most severe persecutions were those of Decius and Diocletian. The constancy and faithfulness of the Christians in martyrdom became a powerful means of winning new disciples. As Tertullian said: " The blood of the martyrs is seed."

## The Church Honoured

With the conversion of Constantine, the Church sprang from disgrace to honour. Splendid churches were built, and bishops became powerful. But the Church became torn with theological controversies and sought to define its faith in creeds. Even its divisions led to the spread of Christianity. The Nestorians, condemned and rejected in the west, turned to the east and sent missionaries as far as China, where the " Luminous Religion " secured a footing and continued for several centuries.

Nor was the Western Church lacking in missionary zeal. In Britain there had been Christians from the second or third century. But with the coming of invaders the Britons had been driven to the west and the newcomers were unevangelized. In the fourth century, St. Patrick evangelized Ireland, and from Ireland St. Columba went to Scotland. From Scotland, in turn, St. Aidan went to evangelize northern England, while from Rome St. Augustine was sent to bring the faith to the Anglo-Saxons in the south. In the eighth century St. Boniface went from England to become the Apostle of Germany, and in the ninth century St. Anskar established Christianity in Scandinavia. In the ninth and tenth centuries the Gospel was carried to Russia. Thus the flame was carried from country to country, and there were always those who thought not only of evangelizing their immediate neighbours, but of carrying the Gospel to unevangelized lands. While missionary purpose was not what it had been in the beginning, the fires never died down entirely.

## The Medieval and Modern Ages

Throughout the Middle Ages the same expansion went on. In the thirteenth century Raymond Lull went to Africa and Asia to preach the Gospel to Muslims, until he was martyred. In the same century John de Monte Corvino went to China, and in the sixteenth century Matteo Ricci made a fresh attempt to claim that land for Christ. In the sixteenth century, too, Francis Xavier went to India and Japan. This was the century of the Reformation and the Counter-Reformation, and it saw no lessening, but rather an increase, of Roman Catholic missions. On the other hand, the Protestant Churches were too concerned with their own problems and with the spreading of the Protestant faith in Europe to look farther afield, and for the real awakening of the Protestant Church to the missionary enterprise we have to wait till the end of the eighteenth century.

There had been some earlier movements, such as the mission of David Brainerd to the American Indians, and that of the Moravians to the West Indies and to Greenland. But it was not until William Carey went to India in 1793 that the Protestant world was really awakened to the call to evangelize the world, and missionary societies sprang up rapidly throughout the Protestant Churches. Robert Morrison found a door into China, David Livingstone opened a pathway into Africa, and soon James Chalmers and others were going to the islands of the Pacific. A great succession of devoted men and women poured into Asia and Africa to preach the unsearchable riches of Christ. The social and educational and medical impact of the modern missionary movement would be hard to estimate, and in the history of the social service of men no date is more significant than the beginnings of the modern missionary enterprise. Yet the primary purpose of the missionary enterprise has always been to spread the Christian faith. The leaves of the tree have been for the healing and service of the nations (Rev. 22: 2), but the fruit for which the tree was planted has ever been the glory of God in the fulfilment of His saving purpose, and the sharing with men of every race and colour of the Gospel of God's redeeming grace in Christ.

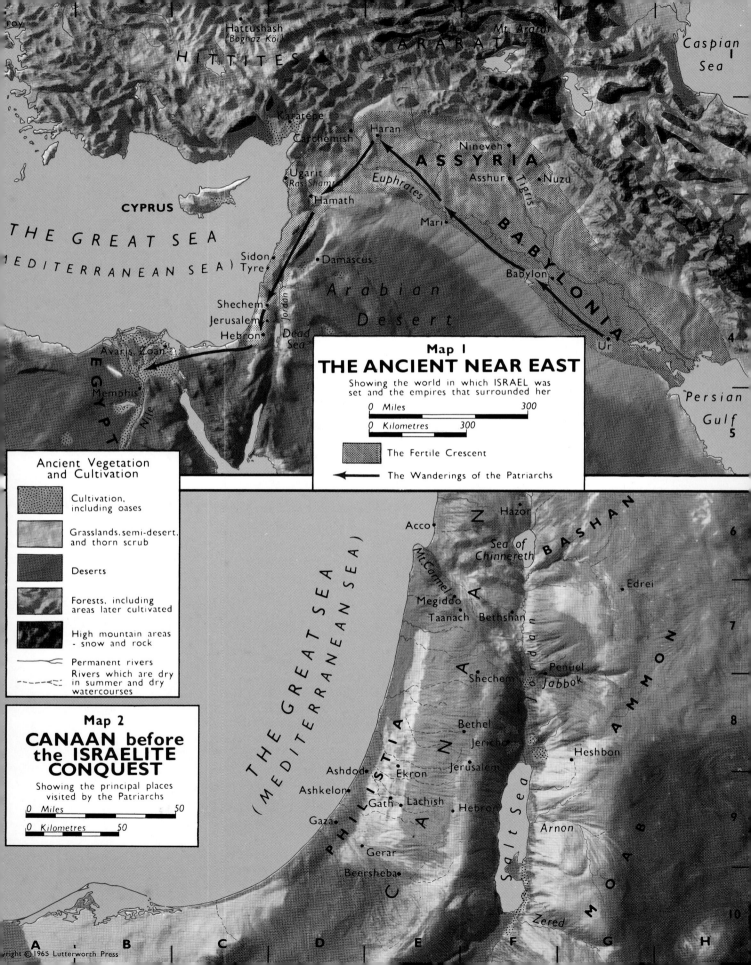

Troy

Hattushash
(Boghaz Köi)

HITTITES

Karatepe
Carchemish
Ugarit
(Ras Shamra)
Hamath

CYPRUS

THE GREAT SEA
(MEDITERRANEAN SEA)

Sidon
Tyre

Shechem
Jerusalem
Hebron
Dead
Sea

Avaris Zoan

Memphis

EGYPT

Nile

Mt Ararat
ARARAT

Caspian
Sea

Haran

Nineveh

ASSYRIA

Asshur
Tigris
Nuzu

Euphrates

Mari

BABYLONIA

Damascus

Arabian

Desert

Babylon

Jordan

Ur

Persian
Gulf

4

5

### Map I
# THE ANCIENT NEAR EAST
Showing the world in which ISRAEL was
set and the empires that surrounded her

0 Miles 300
0 Kilometres 300

The Fertile Crescent

◄─── The Wanderings of the Patriarchs

## Ancient Vegetation
## and Cultivation

Cultivation,
including oases

Grasslands, semi-desert,
and thorn scrub

Deserts

Forests, including
areas later cultivated

High mountain areas
- snow and rock

Permanent rivers

Rivers which are dry
in summer and dry
watercourses

### Map 2
# CANAAN before
# the ISRAELITE
# CONQUEST

Showing the principal places
visited by the Patriarchs

0 Miles 50
0 Kilometres 50

THE GREAT SEA
(MEDITERRANEAN SEA)

Hazor
Acco
Sea of
Chinnereth
BASHAN
Mt Carmel
Megiddo
Edrei
Taanach Bethshan
Jabbok
Penuel
Shechem
Jabbok
AMMON
Bethel
Jericho
Heshbon
Ashdod
Jerusalem
Ekron
Ashkelon
Gath Lachish
Hebron
Gaza
Salt Sea
Arnon
Gerar
MOAB
Beersheba
Zered

PHILISTIA

6

7

8

9

10

A    B    C    D    E    F    G    H

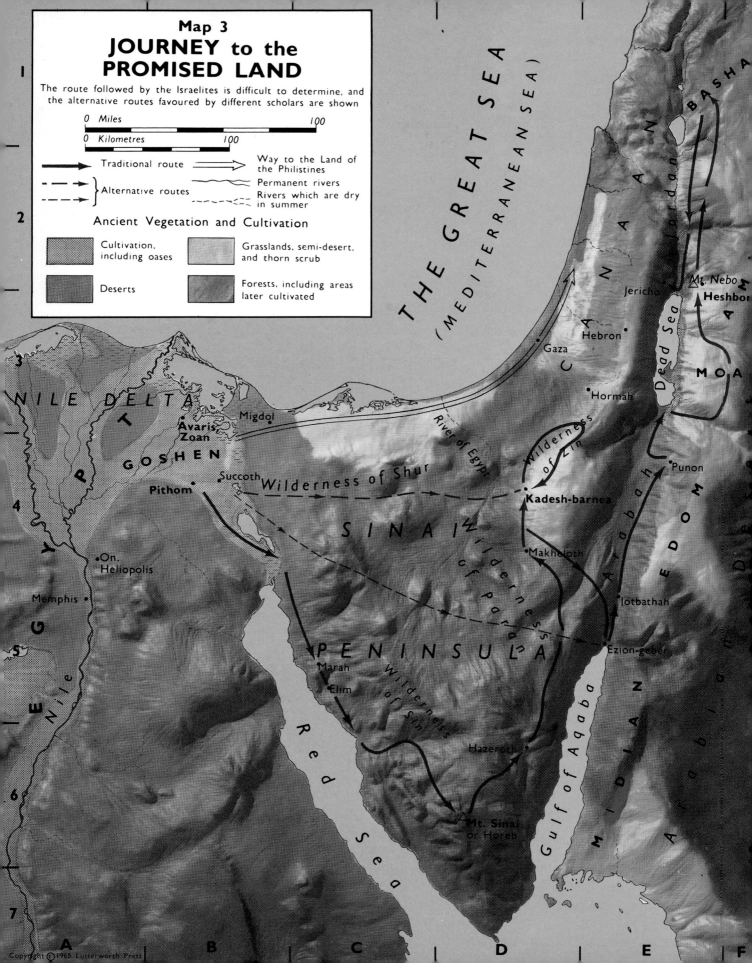

# Map 3
# JOURNEY to the PROMISED LAND

The route followed by the Israelites is difficult to determine, and the alternative routes favoured by different scholars are shown

0 Miles 100

0 Kilometres 100

→ Traditional route    ⇨ Way to the Land of the Philistines
⤍ } Alternative routes    ∿ Permanent rivers
⤍                          ⌇ Rivers which are dry in summer

## Ancient Vegetation and Cultivation

Cultivation, including oases

Grasslands, semi-desert, and thorn scrub

Deserts

Forests, including areas later cultivated

THE GREAT SEA
(MEDITERRANEAN SEA)

BASHA

C A N A A N

Jordan

Jericho

Mt. Nebo
Heshbon

Hebron

Gaza

Dead Sea

M O A

NILE DELTA

E G Y P T

GOSHEN

Avaris
Zoan

Migdol

River of Egypt

Hormah

Wilderness of Zin

Succoth

Wilderness of Shur

Kadesh-barnea

Pithom

S I N A I

Wilderness of Paran

Punon

On, Heliopolis

Makheloth

E D O M

Memphis

Arabah

P E N I N S U L A

Iotbathah

Marah

Ezion-geber

Elim

Wilderness of Sin

Red Sea

Hazeroth

Gulf of Aqaba

M I D I A N

Mt. Sinai or Horeb

Arabia

Nile

Copyright © 1968 Lutterworth Press

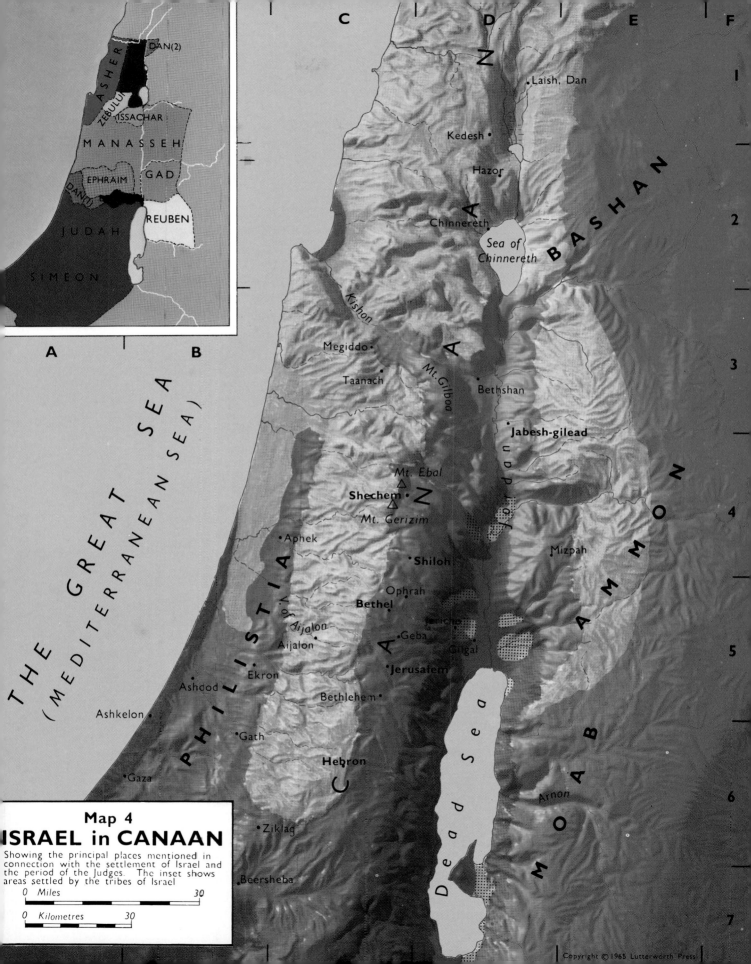

ZEBULUN

ASHER

DAN(2)

ISSACHAR

MANASSEH

EPHRAIM          GAD

DAN(1)

REUBEN

JUDAH

SIMEON

A          B

C          D          E          F

N          1

Laish, Dan

Kedesh

Hazor          2

Chinnereth

Sea of
Chinnereth

BASHAN

Kishon

Megiddo

Taanach

Mt. Gilboa

Bethshan          3

Jabesh-gilead

Mt. Ebal

Shechem

N

Mt. Gerizim          4

Jordan

Mizpah

AMMON

Aphek

Shiloh

Ophrah

Bethel

Aijalon

Aijalon

Jericho

Geba

Gilgal          5

Ekron

Jerusalem

Ashdod

Bethlehem

Ashkelon

Gath

Dead Sea

MOAB          6

Hebron

Arnon

Ziklag

Gaza

PHILISTIA

THE GREAT SEA
(MEDITERRANEAN SEA)

Beersheba          7

## Map 4
# ISRAEL in CANAAN

Showing the principal places mentioned in
connection with the settlement of Israel and
the period of the Judges. The inset shows
areas settled by the tribes of Israel

0    Miles                    30

0    Kilometres               30

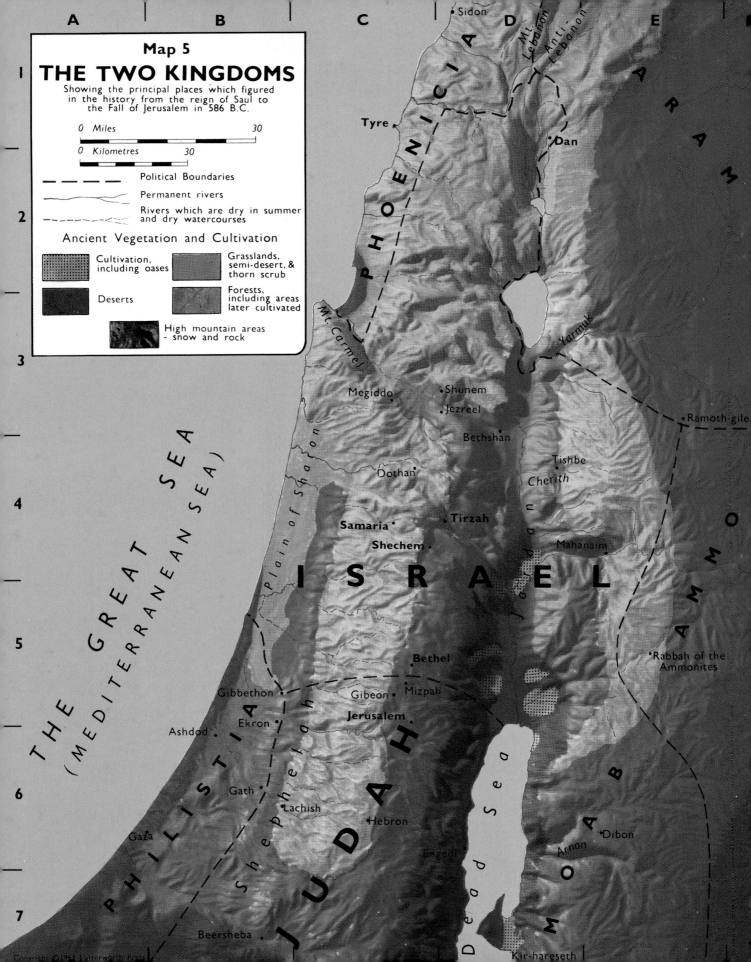

## Map 5
# THE TWO KINGDOMS

Showing the principal places which figured
in the history from the reign of Saul to
the Fall of Jerusalem in 586 B.C.

0   Miles                30

0   Kilometres           30

– – – –   Political Boundaries

⌇⌇⌇⌇   Permanent rivers

- - - -   Rivers which are dry in summer
and dry watercourses

### Ancient Vegetation and Cultivation

Cultivation,
including oases

Grasslands,
semi-desert, &
thorn scrub

Deserts

Forests,
including areas
later cultivated

High mountain areas
– snow and rock

A B C D E

• Sidon

PHOENICIA

ARAM

Tyre •

• Dan

Mt. Lebanon
Anti-Lebanon

Mt. Carmel

Yarmuk

Megiddo •

• Shunem
• Jezreel

Bethshan

• Tishbe
*Cherith*

THE GREAT SEA
(MEDITERRANEAN SEA)

Plain of Sharon

Dothan •

**Samaria** •

**Tirzah** •

**Shechem** •

Mahanaim •

I S R A E L

Jordan

**Bethel** •

*Rabbah of the*
*Ammonites*

AMMON

Gibbethon •

Gibeon • **Mizpah** •

Ekron •

**Jerusalem** •

Ashdod •

Shephelah

JUDAH

PHILISTIA

Gath •

Ramoth-gilead •

• Lachish

Dead Sea

• Hebron

Engedi •

Arnon

• Dibon

MOAB

Gaza •

Beersheba •

Kir-hareseth •

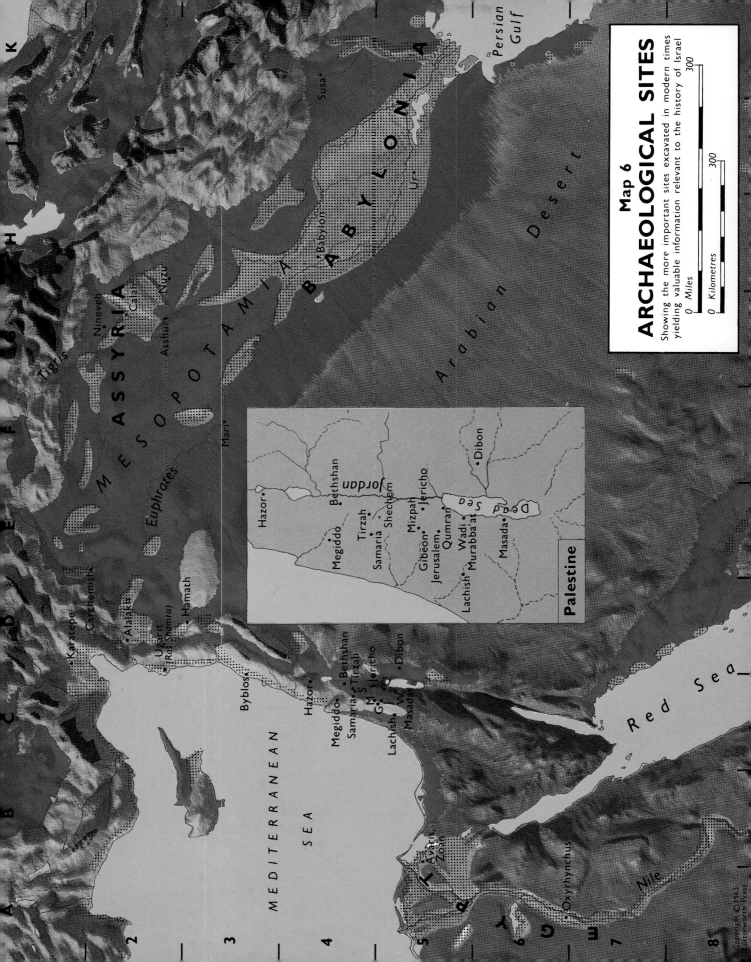

Map 6

ARCHAEOLOGICAL SITES

Showing the more important sites excavated in modern times
yielding valuable information relevant to the history of Israel

Miles        300

0    Kilometres    300

**Palestine**

Hazor

Bethshan

Jordan

Megiddo

Tirzah

Samaria

Shechem

Mizpah

Gibeon

Jerusalem

Jericho

Qumran

Wadi
Murabba'at

Lachish

Dibon

Dead Sea

Masada

MEDITERRANEAN
SEA

Hazor

Megiddo

Bethshan

Samaria

Tirzah

Jericho

Lachish

Dibon

Masada

Qumran

ASSYRIA

MESOPOTAMIA

BABYLONIA

Nineveh

Calah

Asshur

Nuzu

Babylon

Ur

Susa

Mari

Euphrates

Tigris

Karatepe

Carchemish

Alalakh

Ugarit
(Ras Shamra)

Hamath

Byblos

Persian
Gulf

Arabian    Desert

Red  Sea

Nile

Avaris
Zoan

Oxyrhynchus

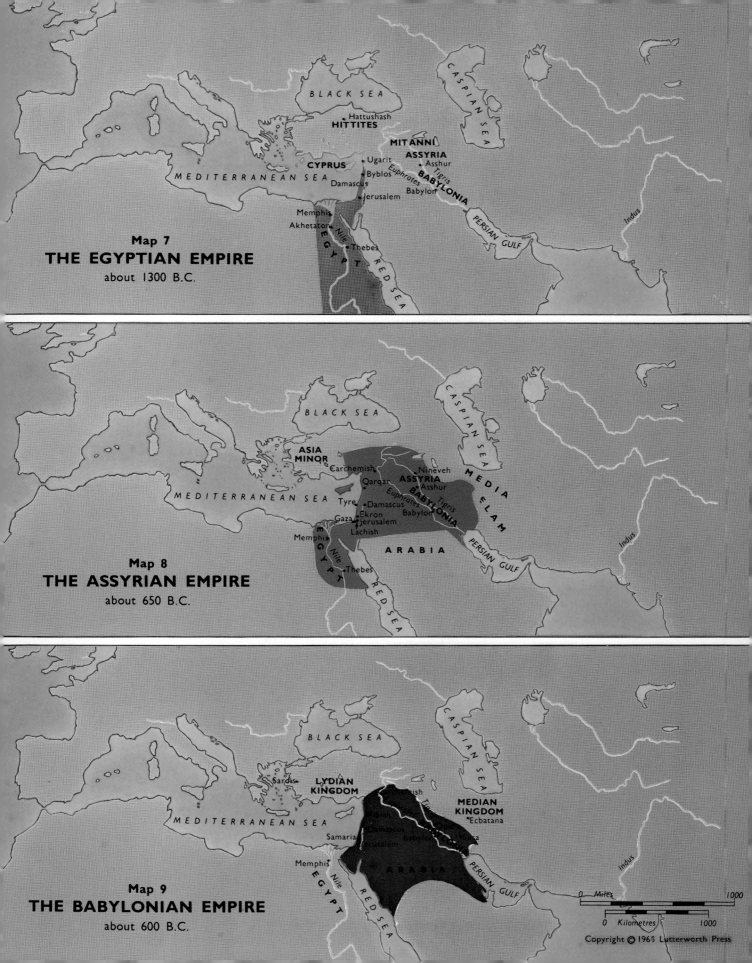

**Map 7**
## THE EGYPTIAN EMPIRE
about 1300 B.C.

BLACK SEA

Hattushash
**HITTITES**

**MITANNI**
**ASSYRIA**

CYPRUS
Ugarit
•Asshur
Tigris
**BABYLONIA**
MEDITERRANEAN SEA
Byblos
Euphrates
Damascus
Babylon
Jerusalem

CASPIAN SEA

Memphis
Akhetaton
EGYPT
Nile
Thebes
PERSIAN GULF
RED SEA
Indus

**Map 8**
## THE ASSYRIAN EMPIRE
about 650 B.C.

BLACK SEA

CASPIAN SEA

ASIA MINOR
Carchemish
Nineveh
MEDIA
ELAM
Qarqar
**ASSYRIA**
Asshur
Tyre
**BABYLONIA**
Euphrates
MEDITERRANEAN SEA
Damascus
Tigris
Gaza
Ekron
Babylon
Jerusalem
Lachish
Memphis
EGYPT
Nile
ARABIA
PERSIAN GULF
Thebes
RED SEA
Indus

**Map 9**
## THE BABYLONIAN EMPIRE
about 600 B.C.

BLACK SEA

CASPIAN SEA

Sardis
LYDIAN KINGDOM
MEDIAN KINGDOM
Carchemish
•Ecbatana
MEDITERRANEAN SEA
Samaria
Damascus
Babylon
Susa
Jerusalem
Memphis
EGYPT
Nile
ARABIA
PERSIAN GULF
RED SEA
Indus

0          Miles          1000

0    Kilometres    1000

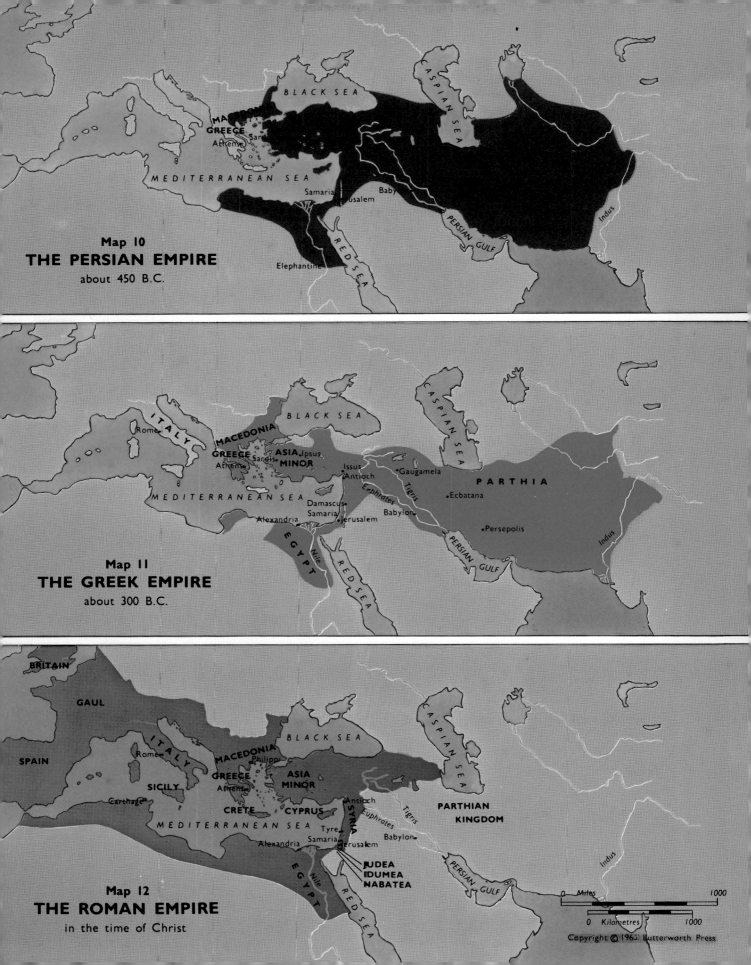

**Map 10**
# THE PERSIAN EMPIRE
about 450 B.C.

BLACK SEA

MACEDONIA
GREECE
Athens
Sardis

MEDITERRANEAN SEA

Samaria
Jerusalem
Baby

Elephantine

CASPIAN SEA

PERSIAN GULF

Indus

RED SEA

---

**Map 11**
# THE GREEK EMPIRE
about 300 B.C.

ITALY
Rome

MACEDONIA
GREECE
Athens
Sardis

ASIA MINOR
Ipsus

BLACK SEA

Issus
Antioch

Gaugamela

CASPIAN SEA

PARTHIA

Ecbatana

MEDITERRANEAN SEA

Damascus
Samaria
Jerusalem

Alexandria

EGYPT

Euphrates
Tigris
Babylon

Persepolis

Nile

PERSIAN GULF

Indus

RED SEA

---

**Map 12**
# THE ROMAN EMPIRE
in the time of Christ

BRITAIN

GAUL

SPAIN

ITALY
Rome

MACEDONIA
Philippi
GREECE
Athens

ASIA MINOR

BLACK SEA

SICILY

CRETE

CYPRUS

Carthage

MEDITERRANEAN SEA

Antioch
ASSYRIA
Euphrates
Tigris

PARTHIAN KINGDOM

CASPIAN SEA

Tyre
Samaria
Jerusalem

Alexandria

EGYPT

JUDEA
IDUMEA
NABATEA

Babylon

Nile

RED SEA

PERSIAN GULF

Indus

0    Miles    1000
0    Kilometres    1000

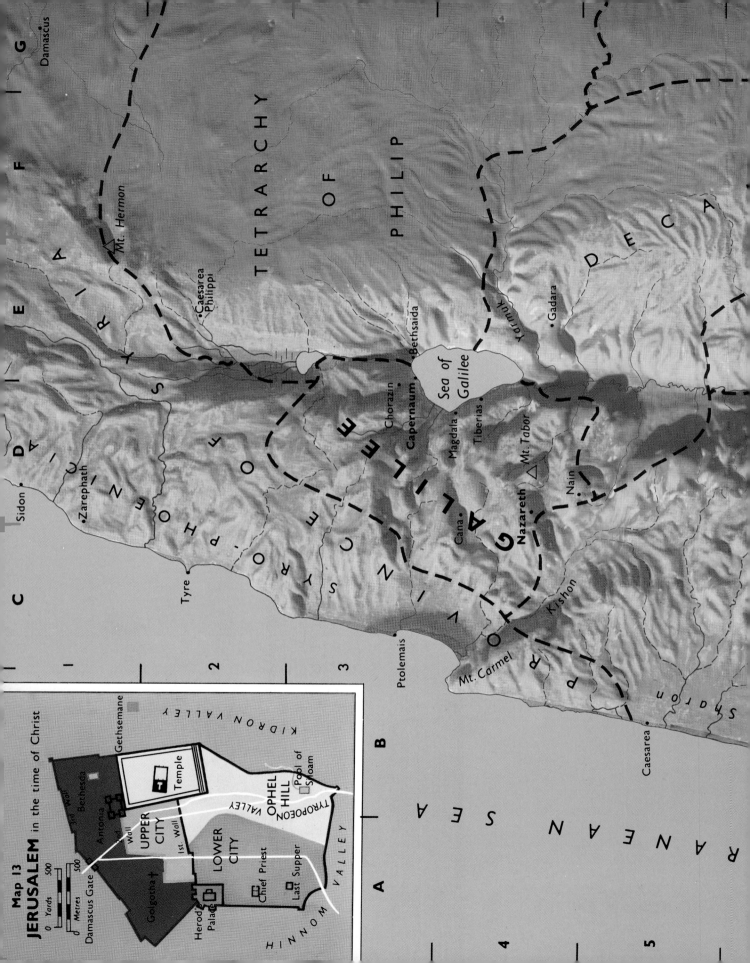

Map 14
PALESTINE in the
TIME of CHRIST

0    Miles    20
0   Kilometres   20

Political Boundaries
Permanent rivers
Rivers which are dry in summer
and dry watercourses

Ancient Vegetation and Cultivation

Cultivation, including oases
Deserts
Grasslands, semi-desert, and thorn scrub
Forests including cultivated areas

MEDITE

Joppa

Plain

SAMARIA

Shechem

Lydda

Emmaus

JUDEA

Jerusalem
Mt. of Olives
Bethany

Bethlehem

Azotus

Ashkelon

Gaza

IDUMEA

Hebron

Beersheba

Masada

Jericho

Bethany
beyond Jordan

Qumran

Dead Sea

Machaerus

Jordan

PEREA

GILEAD

DECAPOLIS

NABATAEA

Jabbok

Copyright © 1965 Lutterworth Press

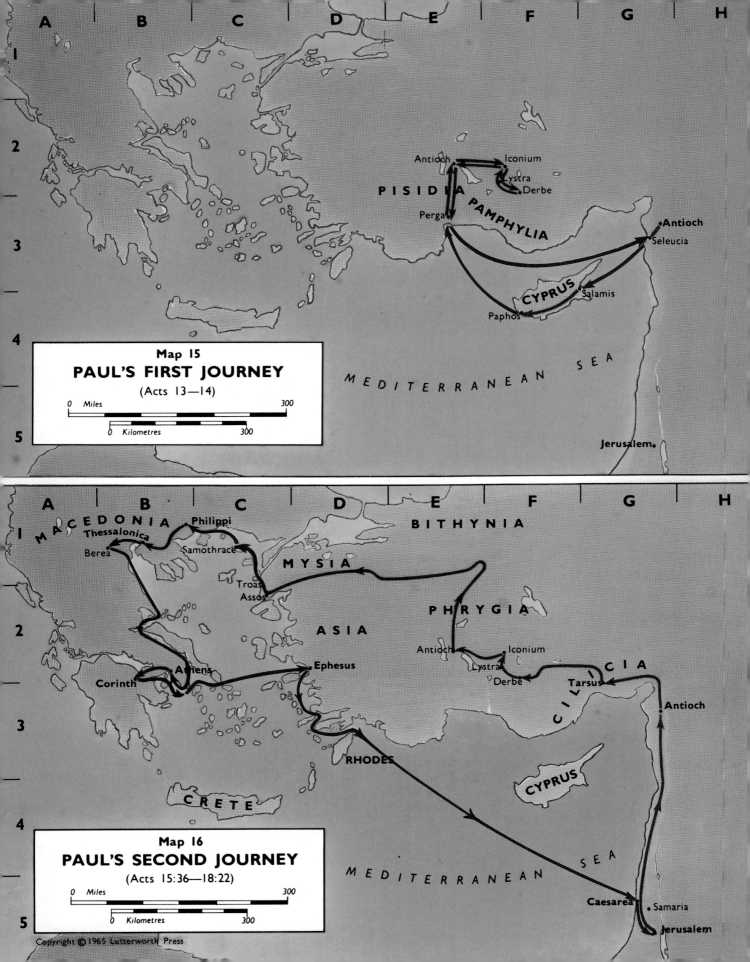

**Map 15**
**PAUL'S FIRST JOURNEY**
(Acts 13—14)

0 Miles 300
0 Kilometres 300

**Map 16**
**PAUL'S SECOND JOURNEY**
(Acts 15:36—18:22)

0 Miles 300
0 Kilometres 300

Copyright © 1965 Lutterworth Press

*Map 15 labels:* Antioch, Iconium, Lystra, Derbe, PISIDIA, PAMPHYLIA, Perga, Antioch, Seleucia, CYPRUS, Salamis, Paphos, MEDITERRANEAN SEA, Jerusalem

*Map 16 labels:* MACEDONIA, Philippi, Thessalonica, Berea, Samothrace, BITHYNIA, MYSIA, Troas, Assos, PHRYGIA, ASIA, Antioch, Iconium, Lystra, Derbe, CILICIA, Tarsus, Athens, Ephesus, Corinth, Antioch, RHODES, CRETE, CYPRUS, MEDITERRANEAN SEA, Caesarea, Samaria, Jerusalem

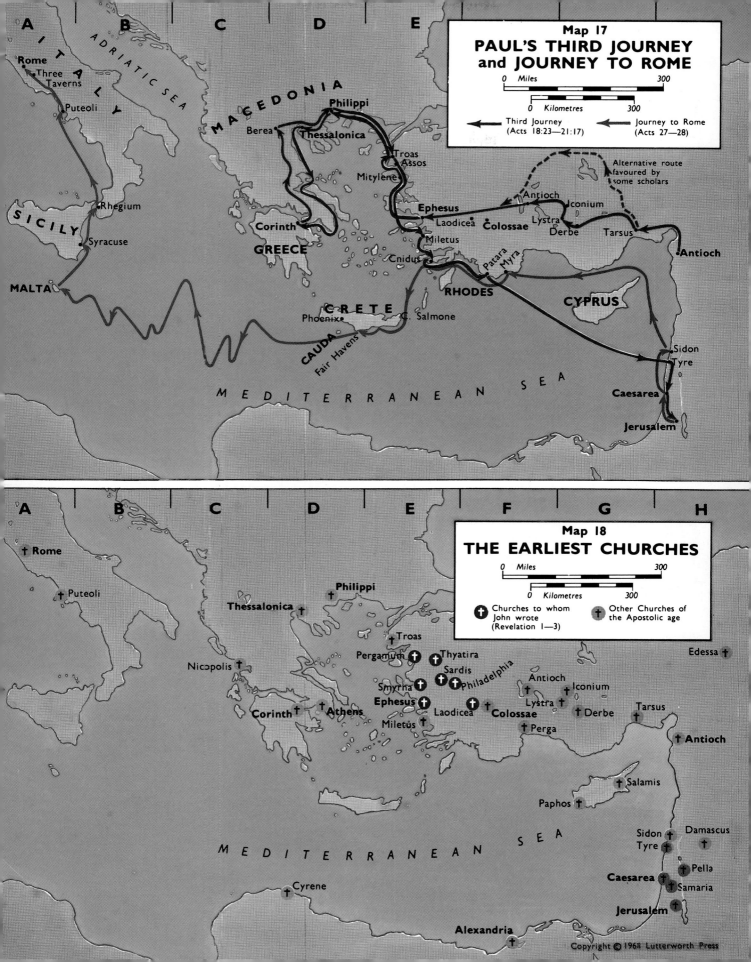

## Map 17
## PAUL'S THIRD JOURNEY and JOURNEY TO ROME

0 Miles 300
0 Kilometres 300

← Third Journey (Acts 18:23—21:17)  ← Journey to Rome (Acts 27—28)

ITALY
Rome
Three Taverns
Puteoli
ADRIATIC SEA
Rhegium
SICILY
Syracuse
MALTA
MACEDONIA
Philippi
Berea
Thessalonica
Troas
Assos
Mitylene
Corinth
GREECE
Cnidus
Miletus
Ephesus
Laodicea
Colossae
Phoenix
Fair Havens
CAUDA
CRETE
C. Salmone
RHODES
Patara
Myra
Antioch
Iconium
Lystra
Derbe
Tarsus
Antioch
Alternative route favoured by some scholars
CYPRUS
Sidon
Tyre
Caesarea
Jerusalem
MEDITERRANEAN SEA

## Map 18
## THE EARLIEST CHURCHES

0 Miles 300
0 Kilometres 300

✝ Churches to whom John wrote (Revelation 1—3)  ✝ Other Churches of the Apostolic age

† Rome
† Puteoli
† Philippi
† Thessalonica
† Troas
Nicopolis †
Pergamum ✝
Thyatira †
Sardis ✝
Philadelphia †
Smyrna ✝
Ephesus ✝
Laodicea †
† Corinth
† Athens
Miletus †
Colossae †
Antioch †
Lystra †
Iconium †
† Perga
† Derbe
Tarsus †
† Antioch
Edessa †
Salamis †
Paphos †
Sidon †
Damascus †
Tyre †
† Pella
Caesarea †
Samaria †
Jerusalem †
Cyrene †
MEDITERRANEAN SEA
Alexandria †

Copyright © 1968 Lutterworth Press

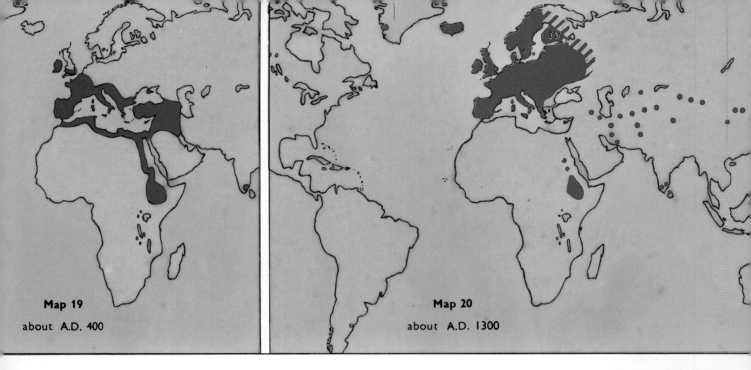

**Map 19**

about A.D. 400

**Map 20**

about A.D. 1300

Map 19. Christianity was not European in its origins, but it spread rapidly among the people bordering the Mediterranean and throughout the Roman Empire. By A.D. 400 it had penetrated down the Nile into Ethiopia. Tradition suggests that St. Thomas established a church in South India.

Map 20. As a result of Muslim expansion only small traces remained in A.D. 1300 of the once flourishing Christian communities in Asia Minor, Arabia and north Africa. By the Middle Ages, however, there was deep penetration into China, along the trade routes of Central Asia, as well as wide evangelization of northern and eastern Europe. At the end of the century there were well-established Christian communities in Malabar, associated with the Patriarch of Babylon; their origin is obscure.

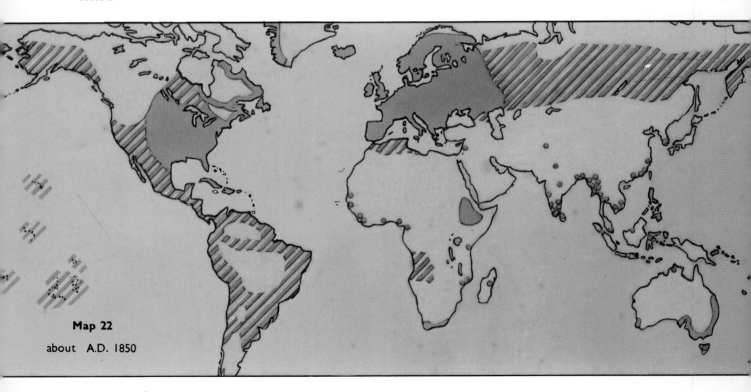

**Map 22**

about A.D. 1850

Map 22. Protestant missionary activity was dominant in the period 1700 to 1850, and extended into every continent, although vast areas of Africa and Asia remained unevangelized. Missions in Africa were confined chiefly to coastal areas; the great explorations of Livingstone and his successors were still to come. Orthodox expansion continued into Siberia and to Alaska.

Map 21

about A.D. 1700

# CHRISTIANITY

Map 21. Between A.D. 1300 and 1700 new continents were discovered by European traders. Settlements were established and missionary work began among the people of those territories. Jesuit missions had penetrated deep into south America, while north America was being colonized by Protestants who wished to escape persecution in Europe. Roman Catholic missions were also active in Africa and Asia, and Orthodox Christianity was slowly spreading eastwards into Russia. Political and other factors caused set-backs in the second half of the 18th century, but even when missionaries withdrew or were expelled the local Christian communities were not extinguished, for example, in Angola, Paraguay and China.

Map 23

about A.D. 1900

Map 23. The period 1850 to 1900 is marked by continuous and rapid expansion of missions, Protestant, Roman Catholic and Orthodox; and by the growth and consolidation of national Churches with local leadership and support, especially throughout Asian and African territories. Christianity was no longer mainly European or western; it was becoming truly world-wide.

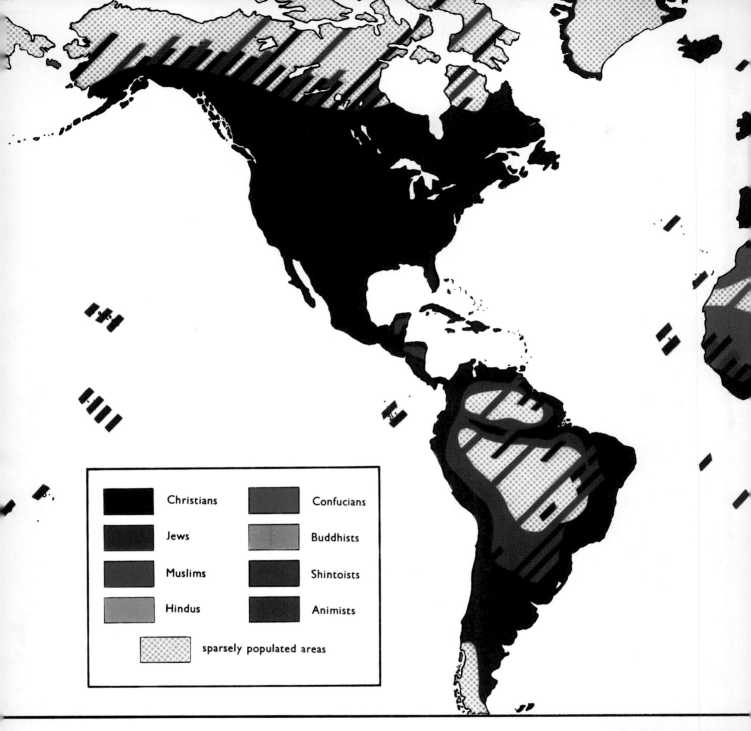

## Key

| | | | |
|---|---|---|---|
| ■ Christians | | ■ Confucians | |
| ■ Jews | | ■ Buddhists | |
| ■ Muslims | | ■ Shintoists | |
| ■ Hindus | | ■ Animists | |
| | sparsely populated areas | | |

**Map 24**

# CHRISTIANITY AND OTHER MAJOR

Maps 19 to 23 on the previous pages show the gradual spread of Christianity at five periods of history, up to a century ago; and a chart on the page following explains diagrammatically how the Church has grown and some of the setbacks it has suffered. The time of its greatest expansion was from the mid-nineteenth century to the outbreak of the First World War in 1914.

This map is diagrammatic in form. The major religions of the world, in the main areas where they are found, are indicated by means of colours shown in the key above. Small minority groups (for instance, Jewish people who are widely scattered throughout the world) cannot be represented on a map of this scale. The colour markings do not refer to precise locations but indicate the presence of the particular religion within the area.

The period since 1900 to the present day has witnessed events that have profoundly affected the spread of Christianity. The world has been torn by numerous wars and political unrest. Secularism has gained ground, particularly in predominantly Christian countries. Other religions have intensified their missionary activities, and especially noteworthy has been the resurgence of Islam. Many countries have won their independence, and travel and communication have brought people closer together. Films, radio and television, books, newspapers and magazines have vastly increased the exchange of ideas, all of which present Christianity with new opportunities as well as a new challenge.

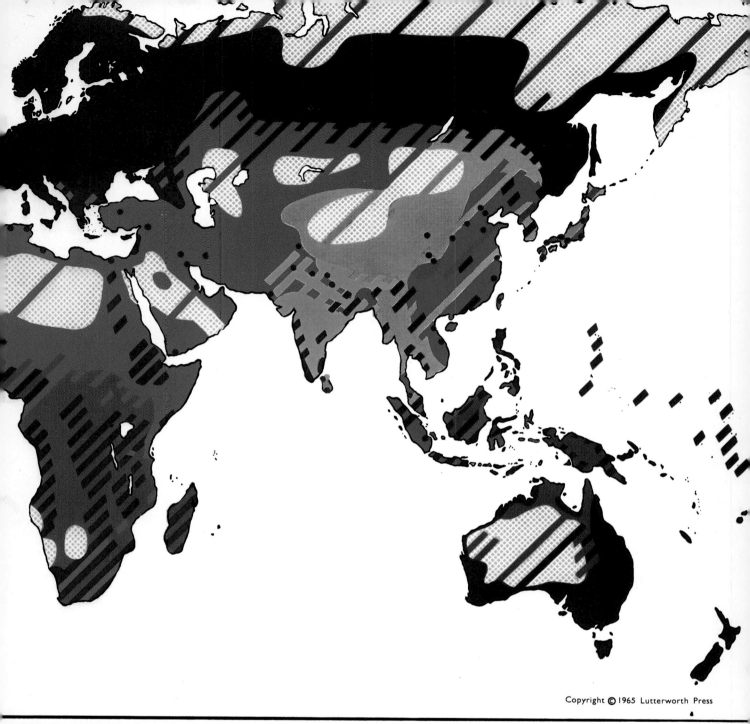

# RELIGIONS OF THE WORLD

Countries which have gained their independence have developed not only in the political and economic fields, but also in church affairs. The ecumenical movement has made great strides forward since 1910, and particularly since the formation of the World Council of Churches in 1948 at Amsterdam. Plans for church union have been actively considered in many lands and in some cases (e.g., India and Canada) United Churches have come into being. Since the Vatican Council in the early sixties there have been many changes in the Roman Catholic Church and much closer co-operation between Catholics and Protestants.

Although there has not been a great advance in the spread of Christianity over the last fifty years there has been no falling off in mission activity. The younger churches show both vitality and growth. In Asia there are exchanges of personnel through Christian Councils. In Africa we see the rise of independent indigenous churches. In South America the churches have addressed themselves to the struggles of the people. In Russia the churches have not only survived the Communist Revolution but have shown signs of growth, and renewal of contact with China indicates that the church is still very much alive there also. Though Christianity may not yet be the faith by which the majority of people in this world live, it is nevertheless firmly established in every part of the globe.

# THE BIBLE AND THE CHURCH
# TIME DIAGRAMS

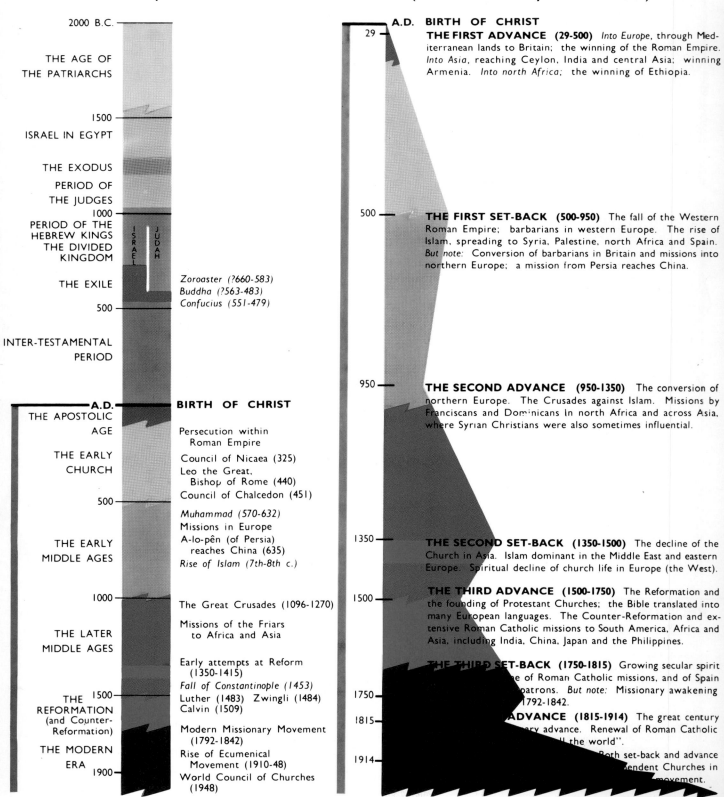

## Chart I
### HISTORICAL PERIODS
**with some important events**

2000 B.C.

THE AGE OF
THE PATRIARCHS

1500

ISRAEL IN EGYPT

THE EXODUS

PERIOD OF
THE JUDGES

1000

PERIOD OF THE
HEBREW KINGS
THE DIVIDED
KINGDOM

ISRAEL · JUDAH

THE EXILE

Zoroaster (?660-583)
Buddha (?563-483)
Confucius (551-479)

500

INTER-TESTAMENTAL
PERIOD

**A.D.**

THE APOSTOLIC
AGE

**BIRTH OF CHRIST**

Persecution within
Roman Empire

THE EARLY
CHURCH

Council of Nicaea (325)
Leo the Great,
Bishop of Rome (440)
Council of Chalcedon (451)

500

Muhammad (570-632)
Missions in Europe
A-lo-pên (of Persia)
reaches China (635)
Rise of Islam (7th-8th c.)

THE EARLY
MIDDLE AGES

1000

The Great Crusades (1096-1270)

THE LATER
MIDDLE AGES

Missions of the Friars
to Africa and Asia

Early attempts at Reform
(1350-1415)
Fall of Constantinople (1453)

THE
1500
REFORMATION
(and Counter-
Reformation)

Luther (1483) Zwingli (1484)
Calvin (1509)

Modern Missionary Movement
(1792-1842)

THE MODERN
ERA

Rise of Ecumenical
Movement (1910-48)

1900

World Council of Churches
(1948)

## Chart 2
### CHURCH ADVANCE AND SET-BACK
**(Based on studies by K.S. Latourette)**

A.D. **BIRTH OF CHRIST**

29

**THE FIRST ADVANCE (29-500)** *Into Europe,* through Mediterranean lands to Britain; the winning of the Roman Empire. *Into Asia,* reaching Ceylon, India and central Asia; winning Armenia. *Into north Africa;* the winning of Ethiopia.

500

**THE FIRST SET-BACK (500-950)** The fall of the Western Roman Empire; barbarians in western Europe. The rise of Islam, spreading to Syria, Palestine, north Africa and Spain. *But note:* Conversion of barbarians in Britain and missions into northern Europe; a mission from Persia reaches China.

950

**THE SECOND ADVANCE (950-1350)** The conversion of northern Europe. The Crusades against Islam. Missions by Franciscans and Dominicans in north Africa and across Asia, where Syrian Christians were also sometimes influential.

1350

**THE SECOND SET-BACK (1350-1500)** The decline of the Church in Asia. Islam dominant in the Middle East and eastern Europe. Spiritual decline of church life in Europe (the West).

1500

**THE THIRD ADVANCE (1500-1750)** The Reformation and the founding of Protestant Churches; the Bible translated into many European languages. The Counter-Reformation and extensive Roman Catholic missions to South America, Africa and Asia, including India, China, Japan and the Philippines.

**THE THIRD SET-BACK (1750-1815)** Growing secular spirit. [Declin]e of Roman Catholic missions, and of Spain [as ]patrons. *But note:* Missionary awakening [1]792-1842.

1750

1815

[THE FOURTH] ADVANCE (1815-1914) The great century [of mission]ary advance. Renewal of Roman Catholic [missions. "A]ll the world".

1914

[Both set-back and advance] [indep]endent Churches in [the ecumenical] movement.

# INDEX AND GLOSSARY OF PLACE NAMES

*References to the Maps immediately follow the place names. The first figure indicates the Map number, and the letter and figure provide the cross-reference: thus* **Aphek** (4 C4) *will be found on Map 4 in the square C4.*

**ACCO** (2 C6), a Phoenician city within the borders of Asher (Judges 1: 31), which lay in the plain of Acco

**ACHMETHA**, *see* Ecbatana

**ADRIATIC SEA** (17), called Sea of Adria, which included waters farther S. (Acts 27: 27)

**AIJALON, VALLEY OF** (4 C5), an important valley leading to the mountains of Judah (Joshua 10:12)

**AKHETATON** (7), for a short time the capital of Egypt, under Pharaoh Akhenaton; modern name Tell el-Amarna, where the famous royal archives coming from the 14th century B.C. were found in A.D. 1887

**ALALAKH** (6 C2), an important city in the second millennium B.C.

**ALEXANDRIA** (11, 12, 18 F5), Egyptian city built by Alexander the Great. It had a large Jewish quarter, and the Pentateuch was translated into Greek in the third century B.C. for their use. Apollos came from here to Ephesus (Acts 18: 24), and Paul sailed from Myra and Malta in Alexandrian ships (Acts 27: 6; 28: 11)

**AMARNA, TELL EL-**, *see* Akhetaton

**AMMON** (2, 3, 4, 5), the country of the Ammonites, E. of Jordan. The Ammonites were regarded as kinsmen of the Hebrews (Gen. 19: 38), and were not attacked at the time of the Conquest (Num. 21: 24; Deut. 2: 37). In the time of Jephthah, they tried to conquer Gilead (Judges 11); and in the time of Saul they attacked Jabesh-Gilead (1 Sam. 11). They were conquered by David (2 Sam. 10f.)

**ANTI-LEBANON** (5 D1), *see* Hermon, Mt.

**ANTIOCH** (11, 12, 15 G3, 16 G3, 17 H3, 18 H3), a city of Syria, founded by Seleucus I, and capital of the Seleucid kingdom. In N.T. times it became an important centre of Christian activity. Nicolaus came from here (Acts 6: 5), and here the name " Christian " was first used (Acts 11: 26). From Antioch Paul and Barnabas set out on their first missionary journey (Acts 13: 1ff.). Here, too, Paul withstood Peter (Gal. 2: 11f.)

**ANTIOCH** [in Pisidia] (15 E2, 16 E2, 18 F2), a Roman colony, visited by Paul on his first missionary journey (Acts 13: 14; 14: 19)

**ANTONIA** (13), a fortress built by Herod the Great at the N.W. corner of the Temple; called " the barracks " (A.V. " castle ") in Acts 21: 34

**APHEK** (4 C4), a place where the Philistines gathered to attack Israel (1 Sam. 4: 1; 29: 1)

**AQABA, GULF OF** (3 E5), at the head of the Red Sea, on the E. side of the Sinai peninsula. On it stood Ezion-geber (*q.v.*)

**ARABAH** (3 E4), the name today given to the extension of the Jordan valley from the Dead Sea to the Gulf of Aqaba. In the Bible it is used of this area (Deut. 2: 8), but also of the whole of the depression, including the Jordan valley (Deut. 1: 7; 3: 17; Joshua 11: 2;

2 Sam. 2: 29, 4: 7; 2 Kings 25: 4). The Dead Sea is sometimes called the Sea of the Arabah (Deut. 3: 17, 4: 49; Joshua 3: 16, 12: 3)

**ARABAH, SEA OF**, *see* Arabah *and* Dead Sea

**ARABIA** (6, 7, 8, 9), mainly barren peninsula in S.W. Asia, whose nomad chiefs are mentioned in 1 Kings 10: 15; Jer. 25: 24; cf. Ezek. 27: 21. In N.T. the name is used of the Nabatean kingdom, which extended to Damascus (Gal. 1: 17), but also of the Sinai peninsula (Gal. 4: 24, 25).

**ARAM** (5), generic name of kindred tribes N. of Palestine and of their localities; often translated Syria. Aram-naharaim (Gen. 24: 10, Hebrew) or Paddan-aram (Gen. 28: 2) is the country from which Isaac and Jacob took their wives (cf. Deut. 26: 5). Aram of Zobah and Aram of Beth-rehob (2 Sam. 10: 6, Hebrew) were defeated by David, and similarly Aram-maacah (1 Chron. 19: 6). The Aram of Damascus (2 Sam. 8: 6) is the best known, and is frequently called simply Aram (1 Kings 19: 15; Isa. 7: 2)

**ARAM-MAACAH**, *see* Aram

**ARAM-NAHARAIM**, *see* Aram

**ARARAT** (1 EF1), name of a region in Armenia (2 Kings 19: 37). On Mount Ararat Noah's Ark is said to have rested after the Flood (Gen. 8: 4)

**ARNON** (2 G9, 4 D6, 5 D6), torrent E. of the Dead Sea, flowing through a deep gorge; crossed by the Israelites (Deut. 2: 24). It formed the N. boundary of Moab (Judges 11: 18; Jer. 48: 20)

**ASHDOD** (2 E9, 4 B5, 5 B6), one of the five Philistine cities (Joshua 13: 3). The captured Ark was brought to the temple of Dagon here (1 Sam. 5: 1f.). In the Apocrypha and N.T. it is called by its Greek name, Azotus (1 Macc. 11: 4; Acts 8: 40)

**ASHER** (4 Inset), one of the tribes of Israel and the territory it occupied

**ASHKELON** (2 D9, 4 B6, 14 A8), one of the five Philistine cities (Joshua 13: 3); mentioned in the Samson story (Judges 14: 19), and in prophetic denunciations (Amos 1: 8; Jer. 25: 20)

**ASIA** [Province] (16). In N.T. times the Roman province covered the western part of Asia Minor (Rom. 16: 5; 1 Cor. 16: 19; Rev. 1: 4). In Acts it has a narrower meaning, denoting the district of Ephesus and Smyrna (Acts 2: 9, 16: 6f.)

**ASIA MINOR** (8, 10, 11, 12)

**ASSHUR** (1 F2, 6 G2, 7, 8), a city on the Tigris, capital of Assyria before Nineveh (Ezek. 27: 23)

**ASSOS** (17 E2), a port where Paul embarked on his third missionary journey (Acts 20: 13f.)

**ASSYRIA** (1, 6, 7, 8), the country of a cruel and warlike people in N. Mesopotamia, who established a great empire and dominated western Asia until conquered by the Babylonians and Medes (2 Kings 15: 19, 17: 3, 18: 9)

**ATHENS** (10, 11, 12, 16 B2, 18 D3), the leading city of Greece, and still the cultural centre of the world in N.T. times. Here Paul preached (Acts 17: 19ff.)

**AVARIS,** *see* Zoan

**AZOTUS** (14 A8), *see* Ashdod

**BABYLON** (1 F3, 6 H4, 7, 8, 9, 11, 12), the capital of Babylonia. Here Hammurabi reigned. Later, it was conquered by Assyria. Its king, Nebuchadnezzar, conquered Jerusalem and deported the Jews (2 Kings 24: 1, 25: 8ff.)

**BABYLONIA** (1, 6, 7, 8), a country in S. Mesopotamia. It was the centre of Sumerian culture before the incursion of the Akkadians, who assimilated much of the ancient culture

**BASHAN** (2, 4), a district E. of the Jordan. Here was the kingdom of Og (Num. 21: 33) before the Israelites conquered it and assigned it to Manasseh (Joshua 13: 30). It was famous for its oak trees (Isa. 2: 13) and its cattle (Deut. 32: 14; Ezek. 39: 18; Ps. 22: 12)

**BEERSHEBA** (2 E10, 4 B7, 5 B7, 14 B10), a city in the S. of Palestine, visited by the patriarchs (Gen. 21: 31, 26: 23, 28: 10). It was assigned to Judah (Joshua 15: 28) or to Simeon (Joshua 19: 2). Here was an important sanctuary (Amos 5: 5, 8: 14)

**BENJAMIN** (4 Inset), one of the tribes of Israel and the territory it occupied

**BEREA** (16 B1, 17 D2), in Macedonia (Acts 17: 10)

**BETHANY** (14 C8), a village near Jerusalem (John 11: 18), where Jesus lodged (Matt. 21: 17). It was the home of Martha, Mary, and Lazarus (John 11: 1), and of Simon the leper (Matt. 26: 6). It was the scene of the Ascension (Luke 24: 50; cf. Acts 1: 12)

**BETHANY** beyond **JORDAN** (14 D8), a place on the E. side of Jordan, where John baptized (John 1: 28)

**BETHEL** (2 F8, 4 C5, 5 C5), a city N. of Jerusalem, on the border of Benjamin (Joshua 18: 13), originally called Luz (Gen. 28: 19). It was visited by Abraham (Gen. 12: 8) and Jacob (Gen. 28: 19). Here Jeroboam I established a state sanctuary (1 Kings 12: 29), which was destroyed by Josiah (2 Kings 23: 15)

**BETHESDA** (15 G5), a pool in Jerusalem (John 5: 2). In some MSS. the name is Beth-zatha (so R.S.V.)

**BETHLEHEM** (4 C5, 14 C8), a city of Judah (Judges 17: 7), and the home of Ruth (Ruth 1: 19) and David (1 Sam. 16: 1). Near here Rachel died (Gen. 35: 19), and here Jesus was born (Matt. 2: 1)

**BETH-REHOB,** *see* Aram

**BETHSAIDA** (14 E3), a fishing village on the Sea of Galilee, rebuilt by Philip the tetrarch and named Julias after the daughter of Augustus. The home of Andrew, Peter and Philip (John 1: 44). Here Jesus healed a blind man (Mark 8: 22)

**BETHSHAN** [or Bethshean] (2 F7, 4 D3, 5D3, 6 C4 and Inset), a Canaanite city near the plain of Jezreel (Joshua 17: 16), allotted to Manasseh (Joshua 17: 11). Saul's body was fastened to its walls by the Philistines (1 Sam. 31: 10). In the Hellenistic period it was called Scythopolis (2 Macc. 12: 29)

**BETH-ZATHA,** *see* Bethesda

**BITHYNIA** (17), a Roman province in Asia Minor (Acts 16: 7)

**BLACK SEA** (7, 8, 9, 10, 11, 12), not mentioned in the Bible; in Greek and Roman literature called Euxine Sea

**BOGHAZ KÖI,** *see* Hattushash

**BRITAIN** (12), added to the Roman empire under Claudius

**BYBLOS** (6 C3, 7), the Greek name of a Phoenician city, which has yielded important finds, including inscriptions in a pre-alphabetic script. It supplied Egypt with timber, and from Egypt it imported papyrus (Greek, *byblos*, from which the word *Bible* is derived). In O.T. it is called Gebal (Ezek: 27: 9), and it supplied Solomon with builders (1 Kings 5: 18)

**CAESAREA** (14 B5, 16, 17, 18), a seaport S. of Mt. Carmel, built by Herod the Great. Philip preached here (Acts 8: 40), and here Cornelius was baptized (Acts 10). Here, too, Agabus foretold Paul's arrest (Acts 21: 8ff.); and here Paul was imprisoned for two years under Felix (Acts 24: 27)

**CAESAREA PHILIPPI** (14 E2), a city near one of the sources of the Jordan, built by Philip the tetrarch, and the scene of Peter's confession (Matt. 16: 13)

**CALAH** (6 G2), an Assyrian city S. of Nineveh (Gen. 10: 11), and the seat of the Assyrian government for many years. Here the Black Obelisk of Shalmaneser III, recording the tribute of Jehu, was found

**CANA** (14 D4), a village of Galilee, where Jesus performed His first miracle (John 2: 1-11). It was the home of Nathanael (John 2: 2)

**CANAAN** (2, 3), the ancient name of Palestine, frequently used in the Bible. The name means " purple ", the same as the Greek " *phoinix* ", connected with the name Phoenicia. Purple was one of the chief exports of the area. The name Palestine is derived from the name of the Philistines. Today Palestine is divided between Israel and Jordan, the latter including a greater area E. of Jordan than the Israelite tribes occupied

**CAPHTOR,** *see* Crete

**CAPERNAUM** (14 E3), a city on the N.W. shore of the Sea of Galilee, where Jesus preached and performed many miracles (Matt. 4: 13, 8: 5ff., 11: 23; Mark 2: 1ff.; Luke 4: 31ff.; John 2: 12, 6: 17)

**CARCHEMISH** (1 D2, 6 E2, 8, 9), an important city in N. Syria on the Euphrates, and capital of a Hittite kingdom. It was conquered by Assyria (Isa. 10: 9) and was the site of a decisive battle between Nebuchadnezzar and Egypt (Jer. 46: 2)

**CARMEL, MT.** (2 E6, 5 C3, 14 B4), a mountain on the boundary of Asher (Joshua 19: 26). Here Elijah's contest with the prophets of Baal took place (1 Kings 18). It was famous for beauty and fruitfulness (Isa. 35: 2; Amos 1: 2)

**CARTHAGE** (12), a colony of Tyre in N. Africa, and once a rival of Rome. It later became the capital of the Roman province of Africa, and it was an important Christian centre in the 2nd and 3rd centuries A.D.

**CASPIAN SEA** (1 H1, 7, 8, 9, 10, 11, 12), unmentioned in the Bible, but Eusebius says that some Jews were deported by Artaxerxes III to Hyrcania, which lay at its S.E. end, in the 4th century B.C.

**CAUDA** (17 D4), a small island S. of Crete, mentioned in Acts 27: 16. Some MSS. have Clauda (so A.V.)

**CHARRAE,** *see* Haran

**CHERITH** (5 D4), a stream flowing into the Jordan from the East, near which Elijah was fed by ravens (1 Kings 17: 3ff.)

**CHINNERETH** (4 D2), a city of Naphtali (Joshua 19: 35), which gave its name to the Sea of Chinnereth (*see* Galilee, Sea of)

**CHITTIM,** *see* Cyprus

**CHORAZIN** (14 D3), a city N.W. of the Sea of Galilee, in which Jesus performed unrecorded miracles (Matt. 11: 21; Luke 10: 13)

**CILICIA** (16), an area in S. of Asia Minor, from which Solomon bought horses (1 Kings 10: 28, *see* R.S.V.; here called Kue). It was later incorporated in the Seleucid kingdom (1 Macc. 11: 14). It contained Tarsus, the birthplace of Paul (Acts 21: 39). Jews from Cilicia had a synagogue in Jerusalem (Acts 6: 9). Paul visited Churches in Cilicia (Acts 15: 23, 41; Gal. 1: 21)

**CLAUDA,** *see* Cauda

**CNIDUS** (17 E3), a city on the coast of Asia Minor, mentioned in Acts 27: 7

**COLOSSAE** (17 F3, 18 F3), a city of Phrygia on the banks of the Lycus. To the Church here Paul wrote an epistle (Col. 1: 2), and another to Philemon, one of its members

**CORINTH** (16 B2, 17 D3, 18 D3), an important Greek city, evangelized by Paul (Acts 18: 1ff.), and to which he addressed 1 and 2 Corinthians

**CRETE** (12, 17), an island in the Mediterranean, called Caphtor in O.T., where it is connected with the origin of the Philistines (Jer. 47: 4; Amos 9: 7). It was the centre of an important Minoan empire, and a flourishing centre in the 2nd millennium B.C., but in N.T. times it had a poor reputation (Titus 1: 12). It is mentioned in connection with Paul's voyage to Rome (Acts 27: 7ff.). Here Titus worked (Titus 1: 5)

**CYPRUS** (1, 7, 12, 15, 16, 17), an island in the Mediterranean, called Chittim in A.V. of O.T. (R.S.V. has Cyprus, in Isa. 23: 1, 12; Jer. 2: 10; Ezek. 27: 6; in Dan. 11: 30 R.S.V. has Kittim, where the reference is to the Romans, and in 1 Macc. 1: 1, 8: 5, where it refers to the Macedonians. From Cyprus came Barnabas (Acts 4: 36), and also Mnason (Acts 21: 16), and Paul's first missionary journey with Barnabas began with Cyprus (Acts 13: 4). When Paul separated from Barnabas, the latter returned with Mark to Cyprus (Acts 15: 39)

**CYRENE** (18 D5), a Greek colony in N. Africa. Simon who was compelled to carry the cross of Jesus, was from Cyrene (Matt. 27: 32; Mark 15: 21; Luke 23: 26). So also was Lucius (Acts 13: 1). Jews from Cyrene were at Pentecost (Acts 2: 10). Christians from Cyrene were at Antioch (Acts 11: 20)

**DAMASCUS** (1 D3, 7, 8, 9, 11, 14 G1, 18 H4), an ancient city near Mt. Hermon (*q.v.*). From here came Abraham's steward (Gen. 15: 2). It was conquered and garrisoned by David (2 Sam. 8: 5ff), but revolted under Solomon (1 Kings 11: 23ff.), and thereafter there were frequent conflicts between the state of Aram (*q.v.*) and Israel. Elisha visited Damascus and instigated the revolt of Hazael (2 Kings 8: 7ff.). It was conquered by Assyria in 732 B.C. (2 Kings 16: 9). In N.T. times there were Jewish synagogues here (Acts 9: 2), and on the way here Paul was converted (Acts 9: 3ff.), and here he was baptized (Acts 9: 18).

**DAMASCUS GATE** (14 C8), a gate of Jerusalem, unmentioned in the Bible, probably dating from the Roman rebuilding of Jerusalem as Aelia Capitolina after the revolt of Bar Cochba

**DAN** (4 E1, 5 D1), the most northerly city of Israel (1 Kings 4: 25), formerly called Laish (Judges 18: 7), until it was conquered and rebuilt by the tribe of Dan, who renamed it (Judges 18: 29). Jeroboam I established here a royal shrine (1 Kings 12: 29), which Amos denounced (Amos 8: 14)

**DAN** [Tribe] (4 Inset), one of the tribes of Israel and the territory it occupied

**DEAD SEA** (1, 2, 3, 4, 5, 14), the lowest body of water on earth. Its surface is about 1,300 feet below sea level; it is 53 miles long; and its greatest breadth is 10 miles. Its water is very salty and it contains no life. The name Dead Sea does not occur in the Bible, where it is called Sea of the Arabah (Deut. 3: 17; Joshua 3: 16, 12: 3; 2 Kings 14: 25) or the Salt Sea (Gen. 14: 3; Num. 34: 3; Deut. 3: 17; Joshua 3: 16; 2 Sam. 8: 13; 2 Kings 14: 7). In Genesis 14: 3 the Vale of Siddim is identified with it. Probably this was the now submerged shallow south end of it.

**DECAPOLIS** (14), a league of ten cities, all except Scythopolis lying E. of the Jordan, whose inhabitants came to hear Jesus (Matt. 4: 25; Mark 5: 20, 7: 31). The cities were: Scythopolis (*see* Bethshan); Pella (*q.v.*); Gadara (*q.v.*); Dion; Hippos; Philadelphia (*see* Rabbath-ammon); Gerasa (*q.v.*); Kanata; Damascus (*q.v.*); Abila

**DERBE** (15 F3, 16 F2, 17 G3, 18 G3), a city of Lycaonia in Asia Minor, visited by Paul (Acts 14: 6, 20; 16: 1). Gaius came from here (Acts 20: 4)

**DIBON** (5 E6, 6 D5 and Inset), a Moabite city (Num. 21: 30), rebuilt by Gad (Num. 32: 34), but allotted to Reuben (Joshua 13: 17). Here was found the Moabite stone recording the revolt of Moab against Israel (cf. 2 Kings 3: 4ff.). Dibon is mentioned by Isaiah (15: 2) and Jeremiah (48: 18) as a Moabite city

**DOTHAN** (5 C4), a city N. of Shechem, where Joseph found his brothers (Gen. 37: 17), and where Elisha was when the Syrians sought to capture him (2 Kings 6: 13ff.)

**EBAL, MT.** (4 C4), a height near Shechem, one of a pair with Gerizim (Deut. 11: 29, 27: 4, 13; Joshua 8: 30, 33)

**ECBATANA** (9, 10, 11), capital of Media and a Persian royal residence (Ezra 6: 2—A.V. Achmetha); mentioned in Tobit 3: 7; Judith 1: 1; 2 Macc. 9: 3)

**EDESSA** (18 H2), a city founded by Seleucus I, but later an independent city and later dependent on Rome. It very early became Christian, and was Syriac speaking. According to legend, Jesus wrote a letter to its King, Abgar

**EDOM** (3 E4), the country of Esau's descendants (Gen. 25: 30; 36: 1). Its northern boundary was the brook Zered (Deut. 2: 13). It was attacked by Saul (1 Sam. 14: 47), and conquered by David (2 Sam. 8: 14), but seems to have regained its independence under Solomon (1 Kings 11: 14ff.). Jehoshaphat reconquered it (1 Kings 22: 47ff.), and the Edomites helped him against Moab (2 Kings 3: 9). It revolted against Jehoram (2 Kings 8: 20), but was attacked by Amaziah (2 Kings 14: 7). After the destruction of Jerusalem

11: 25). It is mentioned on the Black Obelisk of Shalmaneser (cf. Calah) and in 2 Macc. 4: 30

**TEMPLE** of Jerusalem (13), built by Solomon (1 Kings 6ff.); destroyed by Nebuchadnezzar (2 Kings 25: 9ff.); rebuilt after the exile (Ezra 5f.); desecrated by Antiochus IV (1 Macc. 1: 54ff.); cleansed by Judas (1 Macc. 4: 36ff.); renovated and beautified by Herod the Great (John 2: 20; Acts 3: 2); and finally destroyed by Titus in A.D. 70. On its site a Muslim mosque now stands

**THEBES** (7, 8), the capital of Upper Egypt, mentioned in Jer. 46: 25; Ezek. 30: 14ff.; Nahum 3: 8. In A.V. the Hebrew form of the name, No, stands

**THESSALONICA** (16 B1, 17 D2, 18 D2), the capital of the Roman province of Macedonia; visited by Paul (Acts 17: 1ff.). The Philippians sent gifts to Paul while he was here (Phil. 4: 16). Thessalonica was the home of Aristarchus (Acts 27: 2) and Secundus (Acts 20: 4), and the place to which Demas went when he forsook Paul (2 Tim. 4: 10). Paul wrote two letters to the Church here (1 Thess. 1: 1; 2 Thess. 1: 1)

**THREE TAVERNS** (17 A1), on the Appian Way, where Roman Christians came to meet Paul (Acts 28: 15)

**THYATIRA** (18 E2), a city of Asia Minor, from which Lydia had come (Acts 16: 14). One of the seven letters of John was written to the Church here (Rev. 1: 11, 2: 18ff.)

**TIBERIAS** (14 D4), a city on the Sea of Galilee, built by Herod Antipas; mentioned in John 6: 23. Jesus paid no recorded visit to it

**TIBERIAS, SEA OF,** *see* Galilee, Sea of

**TIGRIS** (1, 6–12 inclusive), one of the two great rivers of Mesopotamia. On its banks stood Nineveh (*q.v.*). Its Hebrew name is Hiddekel, which is untranslated in A.V., but R.S.V. has Hiddekel in Gen. 2: 14, but Tigris in Dan. 10: 4. It is mentioned in Tobit 6: 1; Judith 1: 6; Ecclus. 24: 25

**TIRZAH** (5 D4, 6 and Inset), a Canaanite royal city (Joshua 12: 24). Apparently Jeroboam I moved his residence here (1 Kings 14: 17), and it continued to be the capital until Omri moved to Samaria (1 Kings 15: 21, 33; 16: 6, 8, 15, 23). From Tirzah, Menahem went to seize the throne (2 Kings 15: 14). It was famous for its beauty (Song of Sol. 6: 4). Important excavations have been made here

**TISHBE** (5 D4), the home of Elijah (1 Kings 17: 1)

**TRALLES**, a city of Asia Minor, near Ephesus (*q.v.*). Ignatius of Antioch wrote to the Church here from Ephesus when he was on his way to martyrdom early in the second century A.D.

**TROAS** (16 C2, 17 E2, 18 E2), a city in Asia Minor in N.T. times through which Paul passed several times (Acts 16: 8, 11; 20: 5f.; 2 Cor. 2: 12; 2 Tim. 4: 13)

**TROY** (1 A1), a Bronze age city, near which the later city of Troas was founded. Homer's *Iliad* has made famous the story of the war against Troy. Excavations have revealed evidences of several successive cities on the site

**TYRE** (1 D3, 5 C1, 8, 12, 14 C2, 17 H4, 18 H4), a Phoenician city on an island off the coast. It was joined to the mainland by a mole made by Alexander the Great. It was a famous trading city (Isa. 23: 1ff.; Ezek. 26ff.). Its king, Hiram, supplied David (2 Sam. 5: 11) and Solomon (1 Kings 5: 1ff., 7: 13ff., 9: 11ff.) with craftsmen. Omri made an alliance with Tyre, and his son, Ahab, married a Tyrian princess, Jezebel (1 Kings 16: 31). Tyre was captured by Nebuchadnezzar after a long and costly siege (Ezek. 29: 18), and again by Alexander. Oracles against Tyre are found in Amos 1: 9f.; Isa. 23: 1ff.; Ezek. 26ff.; Zech. 9: 2ff. In N.T. Tyre is always mentioned with Sidon (Matt. 11: 21f., 15: 21; Mark 3: 8, 7: 24, 31; Luke 6: 17, 10: 13f.; Acts 12: 20), save in Acts 21: 3ff., where it is recorded that Paul met the Christians there

**TYROPOEON VALLEY** (13), (i.e. valley of the cheese-makers), a valley in the S.E. part of Jerusalem

**UGARIT** (1 D2, 6 D2, 7), the ancient name of the modern Ras Shamra, where famous excavations have discovered important archives, including many texts in alphabetic cuneiform writing, throwing light on the cultural and religious life of Canaanite civilization, and of great inportance for the student of the O.T.

**UR** (1 G4, 6 J5), an ancient Sumerian and Babylonian city, once very important and a great centre of moon worship. From here Abraham's family set out for Haran (Gen. 11: 28, 31; Neh. 9: 7). Important excavations have been made here

**YARMUK** (5 D3, 14 E4), a tributary of the Jordan on the E., flowing in a little S. of the Sea of Galilee. It is unmentioned in the Bible

**ZAREPHATH** (14 D1), a Phoenician city, belonging to Sidon, where the widow, whose son Elijah raised, lived (1 Kings 17: 8ff.; cf. Luke 4: 26, where A.V. has the Greek form Sarepta). It is mentioned in Obad. 20

**ZEBULUN** (4 Inset), one of the tribes of Israel and the territory it occupied

**ZEPHATH,** *see* Hormah

**ZERED** (2 F10), a torrent in the S. of Moab, mentioned in Num. 21: 12; Deut. 2: 13f.

**ZIKLAG** (4 B6), a city in the S. of Judah (Joshua 15: 31), assigned to Simeon (Joshua 19: 5; 1 Chron. 4: 30). Here David dwelt when an outlaw (1 Sam. 27: 6, 30: 1, 14, 26; 2 Sam. 1: 1, 4: 10; 1 Chron. 12: 1, 20). It is not again mentioned until it was resettled after the exile (Neh. 11: 28)

**ZIN, WILDERNESS OF** (3), near Kadesh-barnea (*q.v.*) in the extreme S. of Palestine (Num. 34: 3f.; Joshua 15: 1, 3). In the period of the wilderness wanderings it is mentioned in Num. 13: 21, 20: 1, 27: 14, 33: 36; Deut. 32: 51

**ZOAN** (1 B4, 3 B3, 6 B5), the Hebrew name of the Egyptian city of Avaris. It was also known in different periods as Tanis and Pi-Ramesse, and the latter appears as Raamses in the Bible (Exod. 1: 11). It was the royal city of the Hyksos rulers of Egypt, and in the time of Rameses II there was again a royal residence here. The deliverance from Egypt is associated with Zoan in Ps. 78: 12, 43. Zoan is mentioned elsewhere in O.T. in Num. 13: 22; Isa. 19: 11, 13, 30: 4; Ezek. 30: 14

**ZOBAH,** *see* Aram.